THE

E. P. DUTTON |||| NEW YORK

RADIO CITY MUSIC HALL

An Affectionate History of the World's Greatest Theater

CHARLES FRANCISCO

. . . Nellie, Suzanne, and Norma.

Special color photography by James Stewart Morcom and Vito Torelli

Copyright © 1979 by Charles Francisco | All rights reserved. Printed in the U.S.A. | No part of this publication may be reproduced or transmitted in any form or by any means, electronic or mechanical, including photocopy, recording or any information storage and retrieval system now known or to be invented, without permission in writing from the publisher, except by a reviewer who wishes to quote brief passages in connection with a review written for inclusion in a magazine, newspaper or broadcast. | For information contact: E. P. Dutton, 2 Park Avenue, New York, N.Y. 10016 | Library of Congress Cataloging in Publication Data | Francisco, Charles. | The Radio City Music Hall. | 1. New York.   Radio City Music Hall. I. Title. | PN2277.N52R33 1979   792'.09747'1   78-11860 | ISBN: 0-525-18792-8 | Published simultaneously in Canada by Clarke, Irwin & Company Limited, Toronto and Vancouver | Designed by The Etheredges | 10 9 8 7 6 5 4 3 2 1 | First Edition

CONTENTS

ACKNOWLEDGMENTS

A thorough investigation of a place as complex and as magical as the Radio City Music Hall presents the writer with the immediate prospect of a host of difficulties as well as the opportunity for a great deal of enjoyment. I was able to overcome a number of very unexpected problems and reap the pleasure only because of the incredible generosity of the performers, backstage artists, and other staff members who deserve the credit for making the Music Hall the Showplace of the Nation. This book is truly theirs as much as it is mine.

First I offer my deepest thanks to my friend Dee Dee Knapp. If she hadn't asked me to volunteer for work with the Showpeople's Committee to Save the Music Hall, the idea for this book might never have happened. Thanks also to Carol Harbich, Cindy Peiffer, Barbara Ann Cittadeno, Joyce Dwyer, Eileen Collins, Terri Lindenthaler, and all those gorgeous Rockettes. Who could ask for better inspiration? The beauty and readability of this book has been enhanced greatly by the generosity of James Morcom, Vito Torelli, and Bob Coogan, who graciously allowed me the use of their photographs.

A number of past and present Music Hall luminaries enabled me to dig deeply into the day-to-day operation of the theater that I have related within these pages. These helpful friends include: Russell Markert, Duffey Hake, Evelyn Ashley, Earle M. Moss, Sr., Margaret Sande, Paul Haakon, Violet Holmes, Will Irwin, John Dosso, John Keck, Frank Spencer, Rose Novellino, Vincente Minnelli, Bob Endres, and Rita Sears. Gratitude is also owed Phillip Ulbrand and Robert Kaufmann of the Cooper-Hewitt Museum, Donald Deskey Associates, the Lincoln Center Library of the Performing Arts, and the New York City Public Library. Special thanks also to Larry Spivey, agent Julie Coopersmith, and editor Bill Whitehead. They saw the value of this project, threw me the ball, and let me run with it. As the Irish say, *Sláinte agus saol agut!* . . . good health and long life to you all!

PROLOGUE

Christmas of 1932 was less than opulent for most New Yorkers. Even though there was hope on the horizon, most of the world was wallowing in the depths of the Great Depression. It was a bleak time, and those who could afford it flocked to legitimate theaters and movie houses in a desperate attempt to forget their worries.

The days between Christmas and the New Year precipitated an unusual flurry of activity on the Broadway stage. On December 26 Walter Hampden opened in another revival of *Cyrano de Bergerac* at the New Amsterdam Theatre; *The Little Black Book,* a play about scandals in Washington, made its debut at the Selwyn Theatre; an all-black musical called *Shuffle Along of 1933* with music by Eubie Blake and Noble Sissle opened at the Mansfield Theatre; and two-a-day, big-time vaudeville returned to the Broadway Theatre with Joe Frisco and Ted Healy among the headliners. Inveterate first-nighters were looking forward to December 28 when Ireland's Abbey Theatre Players were scheduled to arrive at the Martin Beck Theatre in T. C. Murray's drama, *Autumn Fire.*

All of the openings, however, were overshadowed by an event announced for December 27, 1932. This was the hottest ticket in town. More than 100,000 people had requested admission, but only 6,200 could be obliged. The fortunate few would not only see a spectacular new show, but also be the first to inspect a new theater—one that was already being described as the largest and most elegant ever built. It was called the Radio City Music Hall.

They braved monumental traffic jams and heavy rain, but many of them still managed to arrive early on the night of December 27, 1932. Those first patrons of the new theater knew they were in for a spectacular evening. They had come to examine the fruits of the perfect marriage between the financial power of John D. Rockefeller, Jr., and the theatrical genius of S. L. "Roxy" Rothafel. Rockefeller was demonstrating his faith in the American future by opening this first of a number of new buildings in the sprawling Radio City complex, and the great Roxy always knew how to put on a show.

Perhaps remembering the pandemonium in the streets at the opening of the nearby Roxy Theatre more than five years earlier, the New York City Police Department had taken special precaution to handle the crowds that began to converge on the corner of Fiftieth Street and Sixth Avenue. Two hundred fifty officers had been assigned to the traffic detail in and around the neighborhood. Theater District traffic regulations had been extended as far east as Fifth Avenue. Special routes had been mapped out for those going to the new Music Hall.

But the cold December rain made the traffic cops' job more difficult. Rubberneckers pushed against the restraining barriers near the theater's marquee and Music Hall ushers were recruited by the police to aid in keeping a path open into the building. Many thousands of people huddled against the rain in the shadow of the Sixth Avenue Elevated train platform. If they couldn't afford a ticket, they were determined to watch the free show. It promised to be a memorable evening.

ONE

A THEATER IS BORN

In the early days of American Nationhood, New York City lay far to the south of the area we know today as Midtown. In fact, except for a bustling area at the southern end of the island, Manhattan was largely rural. Until 1801, the ground bordered by today's Forty-eighth and Fifty-first Streets and Fifth Avenue and the Avenue of the Americas was common pasture land.

The land was purchased in that year by a man named Dr. David Hosack, who was both a conservationist and a visionary. With great sailing ships arriving regularly with masses of immigrants from Europe, Hosack reasoned that the city had no direction in which to expand except to the north. He was a botanist and a lover of nature. He was determined to create an oasis that would preserve the natural beauty of the island and expand it into a botanical garden for the edification and recreation of the populace. To that end he transformed twenty acres of the property into the Elgin Botanic Garden, complete with walkways, greenhouses, and a pavilion.

By 1814, the northward progression was in full swing, and the real estate value of the Elgin Botanic Garden had escalated enormously. Hosack's failing health prompted him to entertain an offer to purchase the land. Columbia College, the forerunner of today's Columbia University, was already becoming a force to be reckoned with in American higher education. Columbia's trustees were quick to recognize the eventual worth of the Hosack property. In time the college would need room to expand and the site was an excellent investment as income property even if it were never used for educational purposes. The trustees assured Hosack that his garden would not be destroyed in the near future and the sale was made in 1814. Columbia University holds title to the land to this day.

It seems likely that John D. Rockefeller, Jr., was well acquainted with the land throughout most of his life. His father had built a fine mansion on Fifty-third Street in the mid-1800s and the young Rockefeller had an unobstructed view of the largely undeveloped property from the rear windows of his childhood home. Perhaps it was that familiarity with the area that prompted him to make a momentous decision in 1928—a decision widely believed to be one of the most important in the history of modern architecture and city planning.

Rockefeller was approached by a committee of New York's leading citizens who were spearheading a drive to find a new home for the Metropolitan Opera Company. Rockefeller would say later that he had never been particularly devoted to opera, but his deserved reputation for philanthropy and his keen sense of civic responsibility caused him to listen. At the time, the economic outlook for the nation could not have been better and he decided it was a worthwhile project.

In October of 1928 Rockefeller agreed to sign a lease with Columbia for a good portion of its land in Midtown Manhattan—the very same land that had once sheltered the Elgin Botanic Garden. The major portion of the acreage would be used as a site for the glorious new Metropolitan Opera House. The remainder would be `parceled off to other builders for suitable commercial ventures. Numerous plans were drawn up for the proposed opera house. Many open spaces were provided for in the plans, to continue Dr. Hosack's 128-year-old dream of an oasis in the city center.

There were reports of serious squabbling between the principals of the opera project. The quarrels worsened as the economic outlook for the nation grew shakier. When the stock market crashed early in November 1929, the opera committee felt the general panic and so dropped the entire project.

In later years Rockefeller would tell his associates, "The opera people were unable to finance their building project. They asked me to make a very large contribution to it in addition to making the necessary land available for a public square and street. Feeling that I had done my full share, I asked to be excused. Shortly thereafter because of financial and legal difficulties, the opera people withdrew entirely from the undertaking . . . an undertaking which they themselves had initiated and which I had become interested in solely at their insistence."

From this bucolic beginning rose the Radio City Music Hall and the towering structures of Rockefeller Center. (Courtesy of the Bettmann Archive.)

The collapse of the opera project left Rockefeller in a difficult position, to say the least. He had signed a long-term lease on the Midtown property with renewal options for nearly a hundred years. That lease was costing him $3.3 million a year. With the original plan in tatters, he had little choice but to go ahead on his own. It is to his credit that he decided to construct an aesthetically inspiring city within a city. We know it today as Rockefeller Center, and the Radio City Music Hall is one of its most important components.

John D. Rockefeller, Jr., had already engaged the Todd, Robertson, and Todd Engineering Company to supervise the work on the opera project. Shortly before that undertaking fell through, the engineering company had commissioned the Reinhard and Hofmeister architectural firm to draw up plans for the opera complex. These companies were retained for the new center and were joined by the firm of Corbett, Harrison, and MacMurray. Later the prominent architect Raymond Hood would be added to the staff as a special consultant. Eventually, the combined firms operated under the collective title of The Associated Architects.

Raymond Hood is generally credited with the idea that led to the eventual building of the Radio City Music Hall. Rockefeller's first problem was to find a tenant of sufficient wealth and attractiveness to replace the Metropolitan Opera as the focal point of the new center. Hood suggested that the growing young Radio Corporation of America might provide the perfect solution. RCA not only specialized in the manufacture of radio sets and components, but also owned the National Broadcasting Company as well as RKO, one of the leading motion-picture studios and distributing companies.

David Sarnoff was the head of RCA, and his NBC radio programs were attracting huge audiences and having an ever-increasing impact on the everyday life of the American people. Chief among his NBC stars was S. L. Rothafel, or "Roxy" as he was known to millions across the nation. Roxy also had no peer in the operation of popular theaters and it seems likely that Sarnoff consulted him before making a decision about the Rockefeller Center proposal. In June of 1930 RCA became the major tenant of the new center by signing a contract for space to be built, including two new theaters.

The Associated Architects drew new plans to include the theaters, one at the corner of Fiftieth Street and Sixth Avenue and the other at Forty-ninth Street and Sixth Avenue. With RCA and RKO heavily involved in the new Radio City, as Sarnoff liked to call it, speculation grew that Roxy Rothafel would soon leave the great movie palace that bore his name to join the new entertainment venture. Roxy ended the speculation by formally announcing his resignation at the Roxy Theatre in January of 1931. The news that he would head the two new theaters at Rockefeller Center proved to be a publicity bonanza. In truth, he would be more than director general of both theaters. His charisma, knowledge, and courage gave him an immediate promotion to "unofficial chief of architecture and construction" at the huge new theater and its smaller sister house. He seemed eminently well-qualified for the job.

Roxy had not been born into the entertainment business or even within the precincts of its capital, New York City. He had been born on July 9, 1882, in the little lumbering town of Stillwater, Minnesota, where his immigrant parents had settled shortly after their marriage. His father had moved the family to the squalid streets of Manhattan's Lower East Side when Samuel Lionel was nearly thirteen years old. Young Sam was quickly sent out to work as a means of improving the family income.

In an effort to please his stern father, young Rothafel held a long series of inconsequential jobs. But he was a dreamer and a rebel. When he was sixteen, his father lost his patience and banished him from the house. He continued on in a series of odd jobs, including some that put him into loose contact with the theater, and at eighteen enlisted in the U.S. Marine Corps, where he was to serve a total of seven years including combat time during the Boxer Rebellion in China. For the first time, Rothafel found something he liked and his new interest enabled him to rise to the rank of drill sergeant before his enlistment ended.

He found himself at loose ends again in the civilian world. He worked at a series of menial jobs until his athletic prowess landed him a spot on a minor-league baseball team in Pennsylvania. It was there, while playing baseball, that he picked up the nickname that was to become his world-famous signature in later years. The local fans, apparently having trouble pronouncing the name Rothafel, began calling their exciting new hitter "Roxy."

At the end of the baseball season of 1907, Roxy decided not to join his Northeast Pennsylvania League teammates in their off-season jobs in the coal mines. He was sure there had to be an easier way, and thought he had found it when he took a job selling books on a door-to-door basis. The position proved to be less lucrative and interesting than he had supposed. But, in a roundabout way, it led him into the career that would make him rich and famous.

In December of 1907, weary and disgusted on a frustrating day of attempted book salesmanship, he stopped in a tavern for a beer and a snack. By the time he had left some hours later, he had met his future wife and got himself a job behind the bar—"where the customers would come to me."

In less than a year he had married Boss Julius Freedman's daughter, Rosa, and was well on his way to opening his first theater—a large room attached to the main part of the tavern. In the past, the room had been used for occasional social gatherings, but Roxy thought it might make a dandy little showplace for the new moving pictures he had enjoyed in the larger towns. Freedman bought the idea and "Rothafel's Family Theatre" opened on Christmas Day of 1908. On the opening bill were a pianist, vaudeville acts, a sing-along, a one-reeler, and special films of the World Series between the Cubs and Tigers. The price of admission was five cents.

The little theater in Forest City opened up an entirely new world to Roxy. He found himself experimenting with lighting, curtains, and all the other innovations his fertile imagination and limited budget could improvise. In time, the news of this unusual operation in a "hick town" in Pennsylvania had reached the right ears in New York City and Roxy was called in to meet with the most important producer in American vaudeville, Benjamin F. Keith. Keith hired Roxy and sent him on a nationwide tour of his theaters to dress up the presentation of films on his vaudeville circuit.

In short order, Roxy's innovative taste and driving ambition had made him well-recognized as *the* expert on proper ways to utilize the new movies as a means of bolstering sagging profits in standard vaudeville houses. His first big personal triumph came at the Alhambra Theatre in Milwaukee where the owner hired him on Roxy's promise that he could restructure the dying theater to pay big dividends quickly. For the first time he had the money and the authority to put some of his cherished plans to work. He installed a nursery in the theater so mothers could catch the matinees without worrying about their offspring. He hired a special staff of uniformed ushers, took out the orchestra pit and moved the musicians onstage, bought new draperies and carpets and lights. He ran over his budget, but the theater went into the black in a week and the owner later sold it at a huge profit.

But Roxy had his sights on the big time; he wanted to return to New York in triumph. He got that chance when Henry N. Marvin hired him in October of 1913 to operate the failing Regent Theatre on 116th Street and Seventh Avenue in the German-American section of lower Harlem. Again, Roxy

(LEFT)
S.L. "Roxy" Rothafel (Courtesy of *The New York Times*.)

(RIGHT)
**This view, looking westward, shows Radio City under construction.
In the foreground is part of the foundation and excavation for the RCA Building
and the Channel Gardens. The tower at the top was to become the new
RKO Building, which fronted the Music Hall. The structural skeleton of the theater
itself rises behind it. (Courtesy of the Bettmann Archive.)**

was the daring innovator. He doubled the size of the Regent's orchestra, instructed them to play *appropriate* music during the varying scenes of the feature film, moved the orchestra onstage amid a variety of potted plants and other adornments, used a luxurious velvet curtain to signal the beginning and end of the movie, manipulated theater lighting in new ways, and quickly turned a nearly bankrupt theater into the talk of the industry. He was on his way to Broadway!

Roxy was named impresario of the striking new Strand Theater at Broadway and Forty-seventh Street less than six months after he had taken over the Regent. At the time, the Strand was considered "in a class by itself," the greatest movie palace of them all. In less than six years Roxy had made the leap from Forest City bartender to producer of the theater many believed destined to become "a national institution." Roxy's star was soaring and he was soon wooed away from the Strand to head another (newer and more impressive) Broadway theater called the Rialto. In 1917 he moved again, to become head of production at the new Rivoli Theater, which was bigger and more glittering than either the Strand or the Rialto.

Each new theater became the scene of Roxy triumphs that overshadowed those in the old. In theatrical parlance, he was continually trying to "top" himself . . . a practice that would ultimately lead to his downfall. Both press and public were surprised when he was not named impresario of the Capitol Theatre when it was built in 1919. (Later, however, he was summoned to save it after the 5,300-seat house floundered so badly it had become known as the White Elephant of Broadway.) With Roxy at the helm, the Capitol reopened on June 4, 1920, with a program called the "Newest, Latest Rothafel Motion Picture-and-Music Entertainment, under the Personal Supervision of S. L. Rothafel."

There was no end to Samuel Lionel Rothafel's showmanship. In November of 1922 he startled the entertainment world and delighted millions of fans by jumping feetfirst into a brand-new medium. He stood backstage at the Capitol Theatre and gave a running commentary on the stage show in progress via Radio Station WEAF. It was the first time a popular stage show had ever been broadcast and Roxy became an immediate pioneer of the fledgling broadcast industry. Within a short period of time, Roxy had set up a broadcast studio in the basement of the Capitol and was starring in the very first broadcast variety show. As stations began to form network affiliations, Roxy became a legitimate radio star and his company, "Roxy's Gang," grew to national fame.

Rothafel continued on at the Capitol Theatre until July 26, 1925. On that evening he surprised his radio audience and members of his "Gang" by announcing that the current show would be the final one in his long series of Sunday evening programs. He was moving on to greener pastures. He turned the program over to his Capitol boss, Major Edward J. Bowes, who would later become nationally famous as host of "Major Bowes' Amateur Hour." Roxy had agreed to go to work for a new theater with a guarantee of a fabulous salary, stock in the corporation, and the privilege of having the theater named in his honor.

The Roxy Theatre, boasting the biggest seating capacity and most ornate decoration of any theater anywhere, had its grand opening on March 11, 1927. Parts of the first production were strikingly similar to those employed at the Music Hall opening five and a half years later. The Roxy program included a solitary figure reading the Invocation and a tableau honoring Francis Scott Key and "The Star-Spangled Banner." It was a smash hit and the theater continued to do well for many years.

Roxy had earned his reputation as *the* expert on popular theaters and he immediately set about to create a theater in Rockefeller Center that would be quite simply the largest and most spectacular in the world. He was not at all hesitant to make his ideas known to The Associated Architects. That brilliant assemblage of talent included the young Edward Durell Stone, who was named design supervisor for the Music Hall.

Roxy confers with a youthful Nelson
Rockefeller at the Otis Elevator Company
in Yonkers where the mammoth
new stage lifts were being manufactured
in July of 1931.
(Courtesy of *The New York Times.*)

Sculptor William Zorach works on
his "The Dancing Girl" planned to grace
the Grand Lounge of the new theater.
(Courtesy of the library, Donald
Deskey Archive, Cooper-Hewitt Museum:
Smithsonian Institution.)

Studying the records of the time, there is little doubt that Roxy (with John D. Rockefeller's approval) was the guiding force behind the final architectural plans. His personal imprint on the Music Hall is still apparent today. Long before his own Roxy Theatre was built, Roxy had decided he wanted an auditorium with an oval ceiling that would curve gently down to the floor. He wanted to carry the curve of the stage opening all the way to the back of the house in an effort to obtain perfect acoustics. Roxy also successfully fought a battle to avoid large overhanging balconies.

The outside of the theater wasn't a particularly difficult problem, once the actual size had been determined. Only a small portion of the space would occupy a position directly on Sixth Avenue. The majority of the Sixth Avenue frontage between Fiftieth and Fifty-first Streets would be taken up by an office skyscraper. City building codes prohibited structures above a theater; the height would be limited to 121 feet. The Music Hall would be allotted room for a huge sign and marquee fronting a relatively small ticket lobby, another architectural detail built to Roxy's specifications. The exterior walls of the building would be finished in beautiful Indiana limestone to match the other Center buildings.

Work on the foundation was started in September of 1931. The new Music Hall was to be the first Rockefeller Center building started and the first to be opened to the public. With the foundation work under way and most of the architectural plans already completed, Roxy still kept the promotional ballyhoo going with a grand announcement that he was leaving for Europe to survey the best theaters that continent had to offer. He was accompanied by a regular entourage, including architects L. Andrew Reinhard and Wallace K. Harrison, a large group of NBC officials, and stage designer Peter Clark.

It seems likely that Clark's part of the trip was very worthwhile from a design point of view. Upon his return Roxy announced that he had discovered a great new desire in Europe for really spectacular productions utilizing new stage machinery. He was determined that the new Music Hall would have even better new machinery and Clark immediately began to devise it.

With the outside structural work well under way by the spring of 1932, it became apparent that there was an immediate need for an important addition to the talented team that was creating the new theater. A limited competition was announced for the selection of a firm to supervise the interior decoration of both new theaters. The firm chosen would set the style and mood to be projected by the interior of the finished building. It would furnish the artists whose works would embellish the world's largest theater, then known on the architectural blueprints simply as Theater No. 10.

Four large, well-established interior decorating companies were invited to submit presentations in the competition. It was widely assumed that one of the four firms would win the bid. Two bright young designers, Eugene Schoen and Donald Deskey, thought otherwise, and were added to the list of competitors.

Deskey was probably aided in his task because of his intimate knowledge of the Rockefeller taste. Under a commission from Mrs. John D. Rockefeller, Jr., he had designed a print room and picture gallery for the Rockefeller town house just north of the new theater. Photos of that work show stainless-steel rods, sculptures, furniture, and other artifacts strikingly similar to those which now grace the Music Hall. He had also received great praise for an apartment he had designed for Adam Gimbel, the president of Saks Fifth Avenue. The Gimbel apartment was an early Art Deco masterpiece with Deskey's use of transite, Vitrolite, aluminum, and stainless steel.

Like Roxy, Deskey was born and raised in the wide open country far to the west of the Hudson River. He later moved to California and eventually studied architecture at the University of California. World War I ended his college career and he did not graduate. He worked as a painter for a time after the war and became more and more fascinated by the intricacies of engineering. He began to see a strange beauty in the new industrial machines and material. Like many young American artists, he moved to Paris in the early 1920s and found acceptance of his "wild new ideas."

He agreed with the Bauhaus tradition that modern design should reflect a clean new classicism that would withstand the ravages of time. Deskey attended the Paris *Exposition Internationale des arts decoratifs et industriels modernes,* the title of which was the source of the popular term *Art Deco.* The exposition also convinced Deskey that his ideas were part of the wave of the future.

By the spring of 1932, Deskey had achieved some quiet renown in a very select circle. His peers considered him brilliant and his customers were all well satisfied with his efforts on their behalf. Still, he was not a wealthy man. He later recalled that he had "probably less than five thousand dollars to my name." But he was determined to spend every penny of it, if necessary, to get the Music Hall job. He spent hours going over the blueprints and touring the construction site. The new theater seemed the perfect canvas for his art. He was fairly certain his competitors would come in with lavish sketches and standard presentations. His would be different.

Deskey had been one of the founders of the American Union of Decorative Artists and Crafts-

Work continues on the interior of the huge Music Hall auditorium as the December 27, 1932, deadline approaches. (Courtesy of the Bettmann Archive.)

men. He called on his fellow members to help him in preparing the presentation, in exchange for the promise that they would be used if he won the competition. He also consulted the American Designers Gallery, which he had helped establish, whose purpose was to serve as a liaison between the artist and the manufacturer. He would make a *dimensional* presentation—one that utilized the materials and the fabrics he would display at the Music Hall. He had been told that the general decorative theme for all of Rockefeller Center was "The Progress of Man, his achievements through the centuries in art, science, and industry." Deskey's style was perfect for that theme.

When he was ready to make his presentation, Deskey summoned the Rockefeller chieftains to a special office he had rented for the occasion. They were presented with sketches for giant murals, models of furniture, lamps and other modern pieces, fabrics for draperies and carpets, and a big array of materials—from Bakelite and permatex to chrome and cork—that he intended to use in the various rooms of the great hall. He also explained that he alone was in a position to obtain the services of America's foremost progressive young artists at a surprisingly low price. The murals and other works of

art would be treated as an integral part of the overall design. He assured his judges that the new theater would house "one of the largest private collections of modern art in America."

The selection committee was suitably impressed and Deskey won the job. He was actually commissioned to do both theaters, but decided to turn over the decoration of the smaller of the two to his friend Eugene Schoen. The Music Hall alone was an enormous undertaking and he would be hard-pressed to finish it in the allotted time. Deskey was only thirty-five when he began the project, but he proved to be a master organizer as well as an excellent artist. True to his word, he went back to the American Union of Decorative Artists and Craftsmen and put together a brilliant assemblage of talent for the huge project.

In August of 1932, Deskey told a reporter for the Chicago Tribune News Service, "We hope to impress the customers by sheer elegance, not by overwhelming them with ornament." At a time when theaters were more or less judged by their degree of ornamentation, the young designer had clearly set himself a risky goal.

While Deskey was toiling away on the theater's interior decoration, Roxy was continuing to beat the promotional drum as the months passed and his great dream came ever closer to reality. Roxy was especially noted for the spectacularly rococo design of his Roxy Theatre, and it was never reported to what extent he and Deskey clashed over the latter's startling new approach to theater decoration. It seems unlikely, though, that Rothafel could have been entirely in accord with Deskey's plans.

As the months passed, Roxy became more and more involved with his primary task—organizing a permanent production staff and lining up the talent for the opening production. He leaned most heavily on those who had been with him earlier at the Roxy and other theaters. But he was prepared to go to whatever limits necessary to make the new theater's opening the greatest event in entertainment history. *His* Music Hall would be the world's greatest theater—even if the powers behind the scenes had changed its name. The first name used for the big theater was the International Music Hall, presumably at Roxy's suggestion. To honor his National Broadcasting Company, which would be headquartered in the new RCA Building, David Sarnoff won the battle to christen the big new theater the Radio City Music Hall. The smaller theater was dubbed the RKO Roxy Theatre.

Roxy's insistence on working long hours and involving himself in every aspect of the creation of the new theater began to have an effect on the robust ex-marine's health early on. Roxy had been treated in 1931 for what he thought was a bout of acute indigestion. It was decided not to tell him that the actual diagnosis was a minor heart attack. His family and his doctor had advised him to slow down. But, despite his good intentions, his fertile brain kept his body driving at an ever-faster pace.

In the final weeks before the grand opening, he was bothered by a case of acute prostatitis and was forced to keep a trained nurse by his side as he went about the business of whipping his giant production into shape. He was concerned only with his theater. Nothing could keep him from the most glorious venture of his life which would bring him the admiration of the "highbrows" as well as the common folk who had grown to respect him through his radio programs and earlier theaters.

We can tell from the preliminary newspaper advertisements that he demonstrated no fear of placing his neck on the chopping block. There could be no doubt in the public mind that Roxy was the star of the Radio City Music Hall. Huge ads, proclaiming the December twenty-seventh opening, began

Ready for the public! This early 1933 photo, looking south, shows the Radio City Music Hall with the Sixth Avenue elevated train tracks in front of it and the station over the Sixth Avenue and Fiftieth Street corner. The El was demolished in 1938. The theater marquee has also changed with time. The flag on the right partially blocks the inscription on the bottom of the vertical sign. Immediately below the word *City* was the legend *Direction of Roxy*. Also note the round RKO insignia to the left of the horizontal sign. (Courtesy of Republic Steel Corporation.)

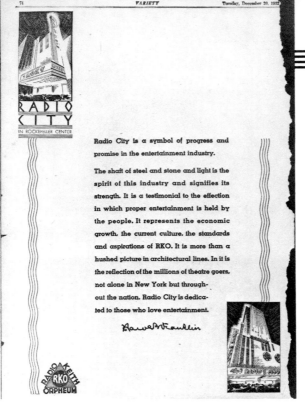

RKO proudly hails the opening of the Radio City Music Hall in this huge ad in the "showpeople's bible," *Variety* (Courtesy of Earle Moss.)

to appear in the newspapers days before Christmas. Many of the ads were dominated by a headline in heavy black type saying, "To the hands of Roxy, master showman, RKO entrusts the two Radio City Theaters . . . Radio City Music Hall and the new RKO Roxy."

The advertisement featured a sketch of the two new theaters separated by the towering RCA Building. Superimposed in front of the skyscraper, between the two theaters, was a photograph of Roxy himself. To the left was a message from M. H. Aylesworth, president of the Radio-Keith-Orpheum Corporation, hailing the genius of Roxy and further explaining the bold headline. On the right of the ad was a message from Roxy. It read:

> *We believe that nothing approaching the Radio City theaters has ever been given to the entertainment world . . . into this crowning work of my life I have poured the best that I have learned in twenty-five years of theatrical experience. With the cooperation of Mr. Aylesworth and his associates; Mr. Rockefeller and his associates; the architects, builders, and artisans who aided in this vast enterprise, we have achieved a magnitude and splendor heretofore undreamed of in the theater. Together with something big and new, accomplished with simplicity and good taste, we have created shows in keeping with their settings—both in the mammoth Music Hall and in the beautiful playhouse which honors me in bearing my name. The same inviting atmosphere which you have come to know in other theaters directed by me—the same spirit of service and courtesy—will here be evident always. In this spirit we bid you welcome to "The Entertainment Center of The World."*

The message was signed as the great man signed all his communications—in his scrawled, handwritten signature, "Roxy." After nearly two years of planning and construction, and some seven to eight million dollars in costs, an American institution was ready to be formally introduced.

TWO

OPENING NIGHT

Roxy stood in one corner of the Grand Foyer as the patrons began to arrive. Close acquaintances noticed that he looked very tired, almost ill, considerably less ebullient than he had on the opening night at the Roxy Theatre. But he did seem pleased at the enthusiastic reception his new theater was receiving.

The patrons were dressed to the teeth—long gowns, furs and jewels, dinner jackets, white tie and tails. The famous and the powerful had come out in force. One newspaper would refer to them as "the most distinguished gathering in years." Former Governor Alfred E. Smith was there along with James A. Farley, one of the key men behind FDR's recent election victory. Many of the celebrities paused long enough to say a few words into the NBC microphones set up in the Grand Foyer. One of them, New York's Mayor-elect John O'Brien, hailed the Music Hall as "the greatest achievement of the theatrical world . . . a new era in the history of New York."

Captains of Industry were there en masse, including RCA's David Sarnoff, Walter P. Chrysler, William Randolph Hearst, and Kent Cooper, general manager of the Associated Press. The Music World's greatest conductor, Arturo Toscanini, was ushered to his special seat. Hollywood was represented by a host of people. Most of the attention went to the well-established star, Charlie Chaplin, and a rising young newcomer named Clark Gable.

Famed aviatrix Amelia Earhart created a flurry of excitement when she arrived, five and a half years before she would mysteriously disappear on a flight over the Pacific. Former heavyweight boxing champion Gene Tunney got a round of applause from the crowd in front of the Music Hall when his car pulled up. An imposing array of big names from Society, Café Society, business, and the arts filed into the great theater. Noel Coward was there, as were Irving Berlin, Hope Hampton, Bernard Gimbel, Henry Morgenthau, Conde Nast, Will Hays, and Mrs. William Gaxton, among others.

The great financier who had dared to construct the theater and the rest of the sprawling Center complex in the depths of the depression arrived with his wife well before curtain time. The chief usher, resplendent in his new gray uniform, showed Mr. and Mrs. John D. Rockefeller, Jr. to their reserved seats in the First Mezzanine. Their twenty-four-year-old son Nelson arrived a short time later.

If the great and near great were impressed with the outside areas of the building, they were overwhelmed by the auditorium. With 6,200 widely spaced seats available in the orchestra section and three shallow mezzanines, it remains the most commodious indoor theater auditorium ever built in the United States. Every seat offers an unobstructed view of the stage with the farthest, at the back wall, a reasonable 160 feet from the playing apron. It is 190 feet from stage to projection booth high over the Third Mezzanine. The gentle curve of the walls and ceiling helps minimize the size of the room, although the ceiling reaches a height of 83 feet at its highest point.

The interior of the auditorium is almost stark in its lack of ornamentation. There isn't a cherub or gold-leafed crown or shield in sight. Indeed, the back wall of the auditorium offers one of the few decorations, sporting a special fireproof fabric featuring theatrical scenes designed by Ruth Reeves. The soffits of the three mezzanines are gold-leafed. The mezzanines are cantilevered from the rear wall of the auditorium, making unnecessary the vision-blocking columns utilized in other theaters. They are curved and relatively shallow, sparing the last rows of orchestra-seat customers the claustrophobic feeling of sitting under a conventional balcony.

The curved side walls of the auditorium are softened by the use of "choral staircases." Roxy had seen similar playing areas in Joseph Urban's 1927 sketches for the proposed Metropolitan Opera House and insisted that they be incorporated into the Music Hall plans. The staircases are actually a series of platforms that rise toward the back wall with the incline of the floor. Each platform has a draped entrance allowing performers to reach them from backstage for special production numbers, which literally brings the stage scenes "into the house."

The great proscenium arch, which soars to a height of sixty feet, frames the stage and sets the pattern for the ceiling. Roxy told the press that he had dreamed up the ceiling design on the Atlantic crossing while leaning on a ship's rail and watching the sun rise. He wanted a lighted ceiling that would create that same vision of sunrise for his paying customers. In reality, an investigation of old architectural sketches reveals that he probably owed more of his vision to the opera plans of Urban, the University of Michigan auditorium, and to the Corbett, Harrison, and MacMurray firm that designed Hartford's Bushnell Auditorium, than to the splendors of nature.

However, it was Roxy who insisted on the curved ceiling—not so much as a design principle, but as a means of improving the acoustics in the great hall. He envisioned an egg-shaped room, ever-expanding from the proscenium arch to the rear of the hall to provide a megaphone effect for distributing the sound from the stage. He wanted a ceiling made of acoustical plaster with concealed areas for the installation of theatrical lighting.

Many plans were drawn and models completed before the end result was achieved. The great ceiling is actually hung from an enormous steel grid that the audience never sees. There is room between the grid and the top side of the ceiling for lighting men to operate in a special concealed booth. From the audience side, the ceiling was deliberately painted a neutral shade to enable the colored lights to project a better effect. With the ordinary house lights on, the mammoth ceiling seems plain almost to the point of dullness. But when fully lighted in any number and combination of colors the lighting experts can arrange, it becomes Roxy's "sunrise" and more.

The ceiling was designed as a series of arches that increase in size as they march from the pro-

This photo shows a Music Hall full house and dramatically illustrates the great curve of the auditorium ceiling as well as Roxy's spectacular "sunrise" effect. (Herbert Gehr, Life Magazine © 1942, Time, Inc.)

Rain and traffic had a definite effect on the arrival time of the first-nighters. This opening-night photograph shows the glowing new auditorium less than half full as the scheduled curtain time approached. (Courtesy of _The New York Times._)

scenium toward the rear of the auditorium. Within the edges of the arches are lights for the ceiling and the stage. The only significant ornamentation on the ceiling is a series of functional grilles that mask openings for other ceiling lights and components of the overall sound system including the organ.

Apertures in the ceiling help provide the Music Hall patrons with a luxury that was a marvel of modern technology in 1932: air conditioning. The cooled air, forty cubic feet of it a minute for each patron in the theater, falls in a uniform blanket over the audience. The air is withdrawn through triangular outlets under the seats, and the recirculating process keeps the air purified even though smoking is permitted in the mezzanines.

The vast auditorium was buzzing with praise for Roxy's new theater on that December night in 1932. But it wasn't long before this praise was mixed with displeasure. Roxy had created a beautiful theater, but his customary punctuality was sorely missing. The curtain had been scheduled to rise at 8:15. It was nearly 8:35 before a series of bugle calls signaled that the show was about to begin. But the patrons were forced to endure further delay even after the auditorium was largely filled.

There were doubtless many in that restless first audience who already considered Roxy something of an upstart. After all, he had achieved his fame through a medium that was still considered rather gauche to some of the more cultured and affluent citizens of the early 1930s. He was a "movie" man—a throwback to the storefront nickelodeon operators. Now he was trying to go "legit" in "a magnitude and splendor heretofore undreamed of in the theater." And, after all the advance ballyhoo, he was keeping his first audience waiting.

What really remained to be evaluated was the show itself. A theater, no matter how grand, is just another building without a fine production to make it live. But the waiting time dragged on and the patrons had to content themselves with studying the large program. The weak-sighted were aided in this endeavor by battery-powered program lights attached to the seat in front of them.

It was obvious that Roxy had spared no expense in hiring a superb staff to operate the Music Hall. The program contained a number of very impressive theatrical names. For the opening bill the production staff included: Leon Leonidoff as production director; Robert Edmund Jones as art director; Erno Rapee as musical director with Charles Previn, Joseph Littau, and Macklin Marrow as associate conductors. Those gentlemen were given their own staff of composers and arrangers, including Ferde Grofe, Maurice Baron, Desidit D'Antalffy, Earle Moss, and Otto Cesana, and were backed up in the music department by staff organists Dick Leibert, Arthur Gutow, O.A.J. Parmentier, two Wurlitzer organs, and an entire symphony orchestra.

Russell Markert was director of the precision dance line then called the Roxyettes; Florence Rogge was the ballet director; Desire Defrere, the director of opera; Leon Rosebrook, director of the chorus; and technical supervisors included Stage Manager Bill Stern (who in later years would become a famous radio sportscaster), Electrical Engineer Eugene Braun, Chief Sound Engineer Harry Hiller, and Hattie Rogge, in charge of costumes. James H. Turner headed up Roxy's administrative staff as chief of administration. He was aided by Charles W. Griswold as manager of theaters and Martha L. Wilchinski as director of publicity. David P. Canavan was in charge of maintenance and Anne Beckerle, R.N., was supervisor of hospitals.

Roxy was already known as the master of the spectacular, and that sizable list of assistants was instructed to turn out the most spectacular and eclectic production ever staged. The maestro himself had combed Broadway and Europe as well as his own personal files to come up with the performing artists, and he signed a large and varied group of them for the opening show.

The 1932 opening-night program documents the size of what must have been the biggest variety or vaudeville show in history. Nineteen separate acts were scheduled, although the size of the bill must have worried Roxy even before the opening. There was a special note in the program saying, "Every effort will be made to adhere to the program outlined above, but due to its magnitude it is necessarily subject to alteration or change of routine." In the end, it hadn't been altered enough.

It was nearly nine o'clock when the program began. Members of that original performing company say today that the show had been rehearsed to run approximately two and a half hours. A study of the program illustrates the near impossibility of achieving so short a running time in actual production before a standing-room-only house of 6,200. Nobody involved remembers the precise running time today, but all agree that it was painfully long.

Roxy, nervous and upset because a large part of his audience had been held up by the rain and heavy traffic, tried to make use of the delay by a hurried consultation with his technicians backstage. He was desperate to get the show under way. He finally signaled his squad of trumpeters, dressed in shiny red satin, to sound a mighty fanfare. The sennet was the cue for Roxy's hand-picked corps of young ushers to march down the aisle in military precision. They filed onto the stage to warm applause which they acknowledged with a snappy salute. The long wait was over.

The opening act was called "Symphony of the Curtains," which Roxy had devised to show off the magnificent contour stage curtain. That curtain, still in use, was the first of its kind . . . constructed under the Ted Weidhaas patents by Peter Clark, Inc. It was so big, it had been transported from the Henry Haug Studio to the Music Hall in sections and sewn together onstage by a huge crew of seamstresses. The great golden cloth is operated by thirteen separate motors through cables sewn into the fabric. In operation, the three-ton curtain can be changed into hundreds of different contour patterns by lengthening or shortening the cables. Utilizing an intricate lighting scheme, the curtain was taken through its paces as Soloist Caroline Andrews performed "Hymn to the Sun" from Rimsky-Korsakoff's *Le Coq d'Or.*

Next came a formal "Dedication" by Martha Wilchinski with Robert T. Haines taking the great stage to the musical accompaniment of two Music Hall organists at the "Mighty Wurlitzer." "Sep-

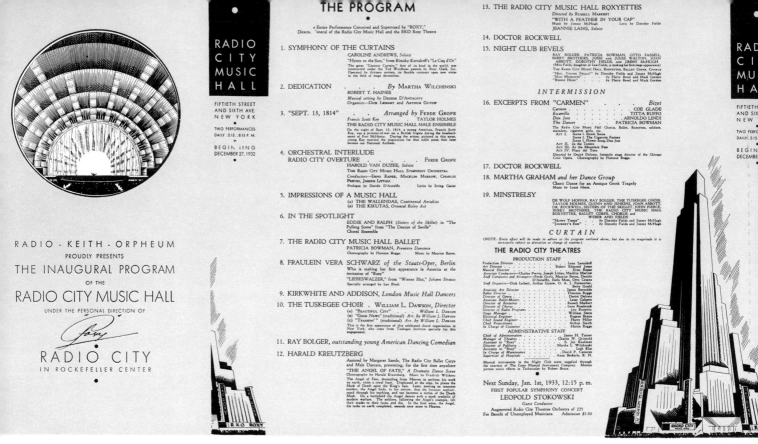

Even the physical size of the December 27, 1932, program was bigger than most stagebills of the period. The opening-night program read like a partial list of *Who's Who in Entertainment of 1932*. (Courtesy of Earle Moss.)

tember 13, 1814," a tribute to Francis Scott Key and our National Anthem, ended the preliminary part of the program. Key was portrayed by Taylor Holmes, and Ferde Grofe, who would later rise to considerable fame in the music world, arranged the music performed by the Radio City Music Hall Male Ensemble.

The variety show proper began with an "Orchestral Interlude" featuring Ferde Grofe's Radio City Overture (lyrics by Irving Caesar) with Harold Van Duzee as soloist backed by the huge Music Hall Symphony Orchestra. For the first time, the audience was able to see the entire orchestra rise majestically on its pit elevator to the stage level.

Moving to more standard vaudeville entertainment, Roxy next presented "Impressions of a Music Hall," featuring The Kikutas, an Oriental Risley act, and the Wallendas, continental aerialists, who continue to dazzle audiences worldwide with their high-wire routines despite the deaths of several of their members in performance. Number six on the bill was "In the Spotlight" with Eddie and Ralph (Sisters of the Skillet) in "The Pulling Scene" from *The Dentist of Seville,* backed by the Choral Ensemble.

Obviously orchestrating his program with the idea of something for everybody, Roxy next presented the Radio City Music Hall Ballet with Patricia Bowman as premiere danseuse, choreography by Florence Rogge and music by Maurice Baron. This was followed by Fraulein Vera Schwarz of the Staats-Oper, Berlin, singing "Liebesswalzer" from *Wiener Blut* by Johann Strauss. A program note made mention that the fraulein was making her first appearance in America at the invitation of Roxy. Another imported act, Kirkwhite and Addison, London Music Hall dancers, was scheduled next, preceding the first New York appearance of the Tuskegee Institute Choir. Under the direction of William L.

Dawson, that famed black collegiate organization performed three numbers: "Beautiful City," "Good News," and "Trampin'," also enabling the producers to display some of the Music Hall's technical effects as an accompaniment.

Ray Bolger, years before he would rise to international fame as the Scarecrow in Hollywood's *The Wizard of Oz,* was the first entirely solo performer listed on the program. He was billed simply as Ray Bolger, "Outstanding Young American Dancing Comedian." Bolger earned the loudest applause to that point with his warm personality and eccentric steps. He was followed by dancing of an entirely different type, a dramatic scene entitled "The Angel of Fate," with choreography by Harald Kreutzberg and music by Friedrich Wilckens. Featuring the Radio City Ballet Corps and Male Dancers, the symbolic mini-ballet was especially commissioned by Roxy for the Music Hall opening.

Russell Market's Radio City Music Hall Roxyettes were a hit with their perfect precision in the thirteenth spot on the bill. The thirty-six beauties danced to the song "With a Feather in Your Cap" by Jimmy McHugh and Dorothy Fields. The next turn, featuring the fake medical antics of a comedian billed only as Doctor Rockwell, was also warmly received.

The first "act" of the program was scheduled to end following the presentation of "Night Club Revels" featuring new performers as well as nearly everyone who had already appeared, incluing Ray Bolger, Patricia Bowman, Otto Fassell, the Berry Brothers, Josie and Jules Walton, Joan Abbot, Dorothy Fields and Jimmy McHugh, assisted by the Roxyettes, Ballet Corps, and Chorus. Lyricist Fields, the daughter of Lew Fields, was making her very first stage appearance. She and McHugh authored one of the numbers in the act, "Hey, Young Fella!," while Harry Ravel and Mack Gordon contributed the other two, "Mad Moments" and "Riding High."

At the intermission it was painfully obvious that the show was running much too late. Those who had fought the traffic and a driving rainstorm to arrive early had already been inside the building for several hours. They had been bombarded with spectacle, music, and dance of the first order. But

Performers fill the Great Stage and Robert Edmund Jones' dramatic nightclub setting during the opening performance. (Courtesy of *The New York Times*.)

they were tired. Many of them didn't return for the second "act," which promised to be equally long.

The second act curtain opened with excerpts from Bizet's *Carmen,* featuring Coe Glade in the title role, Titta Ruffo as Escamillo, Arnoldo Linti as Don José, and Patricia Bowman as The Dancer. The Music Hall Chorus, Ballet Company, Roxyettes, and supernumeraries were in support. Desire Defrere, formerly stage director of the Chicago Civic Opera, had staged six scenes from four acts of the opera.

Roxy had promised variety and the weary audience received it. Following the opera, the mood was quickly changed again by another comic interlude with Doctor Rockwell, before Martha Graham and her Dance Group came on with a choric dance for an ancient Greek tragedy with music by Louis Horst.

The evening's grand finale was called "Minstrelsy," and featured the entire company . . . Ray Bolger, the Tuskegee Choir, Taylor Holmes, Dr. Rockwell, the Sisters of the Skillet, the Berry Brothers, the Roxyettes, Corps de Ballet, and the Chorus. Added to the finale were De Wolf Hopper, Glenn and Jenkins, Joan Abbot, and a young tenor friend of Roxy's named John Pierce, who would later sing at the Metropolitan Opera as Jan Peerce. Opting for a dramatic last billing in the old-fashioned minstrel show was the comedy team of Weber and Fields, whom many in the audience had especially wanted to see.

But a large number of the 6,200 seats were empty by the time the curtain rose on "Minstrelsy." Those who stayed on had arrived on Tuesday evening, and found themselves still in the Music Hall in the early hours of Wednesday—a workday. Newspaper theater critics with early deadlines were forced to leave before the show concluded. One of those was the late Brooks Atkinson, who was destined to become one of the most respected theater ciritcs in the world. Atkinson filed the following report in *The New York Times* of December 28, 1932:

> Elsewhere in these columns appears the news of the fixtures of the Radio City Music Hall and the well-seasoned congregation of guests who assisted considerably at the opening last evening. This department, being devoted to art, inherits the relatively unimportant mission of commenting on the show that Roxy has assembled. Like the enormous, luminous cavern in which it appears, the show has considerable size, since the stage measures just fifty Roxyettes across. But size is no friend to merriment and no great breeder of hospitality. And the truth seems to be that Maestro Roxy, the celebrated entrepreneur of Radio City, has opened his caravansary with an entertainment which, on the whole, does not provoke much enthusiasm. It is more the product of a radio and motion-picture mind than a genius for the short turns and encores of the music hall stage.
>
> Having first conceived of this vast project at dawn on the deck of a ship, Roxy is naturally fascinated by the mechanics and equipment. After you have braved grim lines of guards in the lobby, you are ushered with conspicuous kindness down the long aisle of the auditorium. So opulent are the furnishings that you are played to by two organs that give a perfect sound illusion of being one. The first number on the bill is entitled the "Symphony of Curtains," during which the great "contour curtain," operated by thirteen motors, folds and unfolds relentlessly across the proscenium. Before the orchestra solemnly rises on its elevating platform, Robert T. Haines, costumed like an expensive Father Time, delivers a highly figured dedication, and Taylor Holmes silently represents Francis Scott Key in a tableau denoting the birth of our national anthem.
>
> Once the invocation exercises are out of the way the Music Hall Program finally begins. Roxy has directed it lavishly. Size is his shibboleth. The "Impressions of a Music Hall" presents not

one act of balance but three. As the background of the "Sisters of the Skillet" turn he assembles forty or fifty singers. The Radio City Music Hall Ballet looks like a full regiment when it is finally assembled from twin portals on either side of the house. The Tuskegee Choir, which sings gloriously until the ingenuity of the stage direction drowns it in clouds of Wagnerian steam, is large enough to form a political club.

In such an enormous auditorium the individual performer labors at great disadvantage. Even from a seat well forward it is difficult to have much response to the personality of the performers. Aided by the sound amplifiers they work valiantly and well. Fraulein Vera Schwarz of the Berlin Staats-Oper sings in good voice and obligingly. Harald Kreutzberg performs an elaborately symbolic dance scene entitled "The Angel of Fate," which is explained in the program. But it remains for Doctor Rockwell, the eminent bacteriologist, and Ray Bolger, the dancing monte bank, to establish friendly relations with the audience. Wearing his operating room coat, Dr. Rockwell turns scientific patter into comedy as skillfully as ever. Quackery is a pleasure when Dr. Rockwell delivers it. And Ray Bolger's India-Rubber dancing, which once brightened the "Scandals," is an uproarious bit of fooling. It is a pleasure to roar over his bland and apprehensive stuff.

Since the curtain was a half-hour late in rising last evening, this department was compelled to retire before De Wolf Hopper and Weber and Fields appeared in the last number. Perhaps they relieved somewhat the solemnity of the occasion. But it is hard to be facetious in so large a building and in the presence of such costly decor. High jinks and buffoonery flourish in more intimate surroundings; and, for that matter, princes of display and promotion are seldom cursed with a sense of humor. Although the opening bill is dull, it is likely that Roxy will develop an ornate type of music hall diversion better suited to his tremendous palace.

Considering Atkinson's deserved reputation for erudition in the field of theatrical arts, it seems a bit surprising that he took so little notice of Roxy's attempt to elevate, or at least satisfy, his audience's taste for opera and ballet. It's possible Atkinson didn't expect such a culturally ambitious undertaking on the opening bill. Or perhaps he hadn't grasped the nature of Roxy's artistic goals. His thinly veiled criticism of Roxy, "princes of display and promotion are seldom cursed with a sense of humor," would seem to indicate some degree of irritation with the director general of the Music Hall who had "a radio and motion picture mind."

Earle Moss, who was hired as a staff arranger before the theater opened, remembers the opening very clearly. The management had given him two reserved seats in the First Mezzanine. He had been working on the music for the first show for weeks but had seen very few of the rehearsals, and was looking forward to the evening as a chance to relax and view the finished product.

"There was no denying it was a colossal show," he says. "It had all the elements of a good evening's entertainment—art, humor, ballet, everything. But, unfortunately, it just didn't turn out that way. After the performance, my wife, Betty, and I walked down into the main lobby. For a first-night audience, it was strangely quiet. Like everyone else, Betty and I weren't saying much. I suggested that we go to our favorite speakeasy for a couple of drinks.

"Ensconced at a table and provided with some excellent Scotch whiskey, I asked Betty what she thought of the show. She pondered for a few seconds and then replied, 'I just don't know *what* to think. Something was wrong.' I guess I felt the same way. The whole thing was quite a letdown."

It is entirely possible that Roxy never saw any of the generally unfavorable reviews; he certainly never mentioned them in public. But a showman of his experience had no need to read the reviews. He knew he had failed. He had ignored the advice of his doctor, nurse, and family and had driven

Roxy's portrait in the December 20, 1932, *Variety*. (Courtesy of Earle Moss.)

himself to the point of physical collapse in order to bask in the glory of this night. But the glory had somehow eluded him. He had climbed to the summit only to have the ground give way beneath him.

His position as the indispensable man, the guiding genius behind every aspect of the Music Hall, had been seriously shaken. The seemingly infallible master showman had reached the crest of the wave when the doors opened on the night of December 27, 1932. When the last patron left, early on the morning of the twenty-eighth, that same wave was poised to dash him downward with terrifying velocity. He was literally carried from the Music Hall on a stretcher.

THREE

DESKEY'S TRIUMPH

Roxy's collapse during the early morning hours of December 28, 1932, was no publicity stunt. He was rushed to a hospital and underwent a serious operation on December 31. It would be several months before he would be fit enough to return to a full schedule of work.

There are no documented reports describing the panic that gripped the Radio City personnel in the days immediately following the opening night. The public impact of the indifferent reviews was already having a serious effect on the box office. Millions of dollars had been spent in preparation for that one disastrous night. Worst of all, the knowledgeable, confident leader of the entire project was no longer around to calm their fears.

The executives of RKO and Rockefeller Center, Inc., huddled in lengthy sessions in an effort to solve their dilemma. Had they purchased a "white elephant" of record-breaking proportions? Just what were the pluses and minuses of the situation?

The brightest single aspect of the opening night was the generally favorable, even enthusiastic, reception given the theater itself. John D. Rockefeller, Jr., had paid a visit to the Music Hall several days before the official opening. He had told reporters, "I think the great auditorium is beautiful, soul-satisfying, inspiring beyond anything I have dreamed possible. The lobby is as distinguished and unusual and truly impressive as the theater itself. We visited the various galleries and withdrawing rooms on each floor. These rooms are all of them interesting, unusual, and distinguished to an extraordinary degree. There is a style and chic about the whole building which is impressive to the extreme."

The consensus seems to have been summed up by Percy Hammond's article in the New York *Herald Tribune:* "The least important item in last evening's event was the show itself . . . it has been said of the new Music Hall that it needs no performers; that its beauty and comforts alone are sufficient to gratify the greediest of playgoers."

The RKO and Rockefeller interests, of course, had no intention of turning the mammoth theater into a performerless art museum, but the fact that the building had been so praised was one worry they could scratch off their lists. Everyone seemed to love the building.

That 1932 love-at-first-sight reaction to the theater's interior has grown stronger with the passage of time. Within three months of the opening, an article in the prestigious *Art et Decoration* called the design a "remarkable success." Critics around the world continue to hail it as one of the most beautiful examples of the Art Deco style to be found anywhere. Ada Louise Huxtable, the distinguished architecture critic of *The New York Times,* considers the Music Hall "immortal."

The theater those first distinguished patrons saw on their trip to the Music Hall is basically the same as that viewed by the 250 million other theatergoers who have followed them. By and large, the Rockefeller interests have done a praiseworthy job in preserving and maintaining the beauty of the interior. When carpets, seat coverings, and other fabrics have become worn, they have been replaced whenever possible with the identical material. It is doubtful if either Deskey or Roxy would approve of the large popcorn and candy counters that have been installed in the Grand Foyer and the Grand Lounge since the financial crunch of the mid-1970s. The coin-operated electronic game machines also seem distinctly out of place in the subdued atmosphere of the northeastern corner of the Grand Lounge. But, essentially, the theater has changed little since the night of December 27, 1932.

The point of entry, the ticket lobby, is perhaps the only public area of the Music Hall that is not outsized. It is apparent that Roxy orchestrated it that way deliberately, guiding the patron from a small room, to a larger one, to an overwhelmingly huge one. He had utilized the same kind of plan for his own Seventh Avenue Roxy Theatre several years earlier.

The essence of the ticket lobby is its functionality, its ability to handle great numbers of people

The northeast corner of the Avenue of the Americas and Fiftieth Street glows in this nighttime view of the Radio City Music Hall. (Courtesy of Vito Torelli.)

RADIO CITY
MUSIC HALL
RADIO CITY
ELLIOTT GOULD AND ROBERT MITCHUM IN "MATILDA"
RADIO CITY
MUSIC HALL

15 — RADIO CITY MUSIC HALL, NEW YORK CITY

Photo by Wurtz Bros.

(ABOVE)
The Sixth Avenue El is still visible in this picture postcard
view of the Music Hall, produced shortly after
the theater opened. (Courtesy of Vito Torelli.)

(OPPOSITE PAGE)
Southern facade of the Music Hall looking northwestward
along Fiftieth Street. (Courtesy of Vito Torelli.)

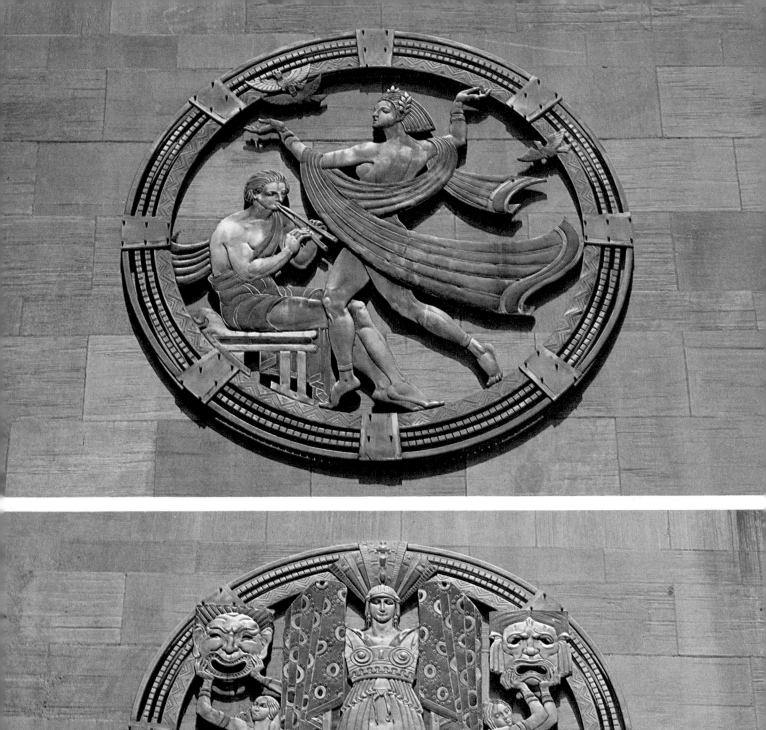

**Huge classical insignia high on the limestone of the Music Hall's southern wall.
(Courtesy of Vito Torelli.)**

These bronze bas-reliefs depicting various forms of entertainment
are usually overlooked in their locations under the Sixth Avenue marquee.
(Courtesy of Vito Torelli.)

(THIS PAGE)
**Bronze-bordered, glass display cases
herald the current attraction on all sides
of the Music Hall. (Courtesy of Vito Torelli.)**

(OPPOSITE PAGE)
**The Music Hall ticket lobby.
(Courtesy of Vito Torelli.)**

(OPPOSITE PAGE)
The Grand Foyer in
its subdued elegance.
(Courtesy of
Evelyn Hofer.)

(RIGHT)
Gwen Lux's "Eve" in
her marbled niche
off the Grand Foyer.
(Courtesy of
Vito Torelli.)

(ABOVE)
"The Dancing Girl" kneels gracefully in the sophisticated atmosphere of the Grand Lounge. (Courtesy of Evelyn Hofer.)

(OPPOSITE, TOP)
The recently-added popcorn and candy display add a jarring note to a Louis Bouche mural in the Grand Lounge. (Courtesy of Vito Torelli.)

(OPPOSITE, BOTTOM)
Interior of a Music Hall patron's elevator. (Courtesy of Vito Torelli.)

Deskey's furniture and the Kuniyoshi mural harmonize perfectly in a third mezzanine powder room. (Courtesy of Evelyn Hofer.)

A never-before-published color photograph of Roxy's studio on the
upper executive floors of the Music Hall. Deskey approached it
similarly to the way he designed the picture gallery for
Mrs. John D. Rockefeller, Jr. (Courtesy of Helga Photo Studio, Inc.)

The small size of the marquee is demonstrated in this photo from across the Avenue of the Americas. (Courtesy of Vito Torelli.)

in a steady flow. It is dominated by its streamlined, bronze ticket booths with windows on each side. A wide bank of entrance doors allows several lines of customers to enter the inner reaches of the building simultaneously. A smaller area, to the right of the main ticket lobby, houses the box offices for advance ticket sales. One of the most overlooked features in the building is the ticket lobby's coffered ceiling with its rows of suspended round light units.

Once through the doors into the main lobby, the majesty of the Radio City Music Hall hits the first-time visitor with an impact that is almost physical. The area you enter is not a lobby, in the classic sense. It is huge, but otherwise bears no resemblance to the lobbies of other large theaters, libraries, museums, or rail and air terminals. This is a *room* . . . a mammoth, magnificent room. In fact, it has always been called the Grand Foyer.

It is easy to imagine the shock those 1932 theatergoers felt when they first saw the Grand Foyer. There simply had never been anything quite like it. Legitimate stage and motion-picture theaters of the period were designed to resemble palaces. Indeed, the great movie palaces constructed in previous years took their themes from exotic fantasies . . . Grauman's Chinese Theatre in Hollywood, the Oriental Theatre in Chicago, the Fox in Atlanta, and even Manhattan's Roxy Theatre were overromanticized replicas of foreign cathedrals, mosques, and palaces the average man could identify with only on his night at the movies. If the Music Hall's Grand Foyer was a room in a palace, then it belonged to a king so modern, so advanced he would have been a king elected from the common people with a no-nonsense, American view on life. And yet the Grand Foyer is regal.

The Grand Foyer, along with the other areas of the Music Hall, precisely reflects Roxy's appraisal ". . . a magnitude and splendor heretofore undreamed of in the theater," as well as Deskey's aim to "impress the customers by sheer elegance, not by overwhelming them with ornament." Here is a huge space with sharply clean lines and soft textures that manages, somehow, to impart a feeling that borders on coziness. Other than the obvious scope of its size, there is nothing in the Grand Foyer to make the average person feel dwarfed or out of place.

That is a spectacular achievement, considering its size. It is possible to stand in the center of the room and see Fifty-first Street through the glass doors at the north end of the space, and turn your head to view Fiftieth Street through the exit doors at the south end. The complete area covers an entire New York City block. The Grand Foyer, proper, measures 150 feet in length. But it's the height of the foyer that opens up the possibilities of its true grandeur. It measures sixty feet from floor to ceiling, a height that makes the two graceful cylindrical chandeliers (each twenty-nine feet long) seem of normal size. A tragic consequence defining the measure of the Grand Foyer's soaring height happened in the early 1960s when a visitor either leaped or fell to his death from the Third Mezzanine promenade to the floor of the room.

The chandeliers, designed by Edward Caldwell and manufactured in his factory in New Jersey, are one of the many striking aspects of the foyer. Each weighs two tons, with half that weight taken up by the molten glass from which they are made. True to Deskey's overall plan, these also stress the simple but elegant line rather than the classic wide spread of shining baubles. Each chandelier contains forty 60-watt bulbs distributed through the length of the lamps with one concealed 500-watt bulb at the base. Each fixture is suspended from the ceiling on an ornate cable controlled by its own electric motor, which can raise or lower it for easy cleaning.

Caldwell also designed and manufactured six matching wall bracket lights. Three of them grace each side of the Grand Foyer. They are made of the same material as the chandeliers, although each is considerably smaller in size, extending ten and a half feet in length and weighing 950 pounds.

The wall brackets, in particular, help accent another one of the striking features of the Grand

Foyer, the six towering mirrors running from floor to ceiling. The mirrors, three on each side of the foyer, further emphasize the height of the room. Wide openings in the mirrors allow patrons to look down into the Grand Foyer from the promenades of the First, Second, and Third mezzanines. The mirrors are also special, having a gold backing behind their three-quarter-inch thickness instead of the normal silver. The gold backing was designed to give off a more subtle reflection to harmonize with the relatively subdued tones of the room.

Donald Deskey, in his passion for new fabrics, hired Ruth Reeves to design the brown-gold draperies that border the mirrors. They weigh two hundred pounds each and blend beautifully with the henna-colored walls that separate the mirrors. The walls are covered with brocatelle, a fabric akin to velvet. That the creators wanted nothing but the best materials in the Music Hall is further illustrated in the use of a special imported marble to cover the base of the walls as well as the columns and other wall areas in the Music Hall. It is a deep but subdued red Numidian Grecher Sanguine marble, imported to the Music Hall from Africa. A careful examination of the finished slabs reveals the superb craftsmanship used in cutting and matching the grains.

The planning and workmanship that went into the building is everywhere evident. The ceiling of the Grand Foyer is covered with gold leaf (at Roxy's last-minute insistence) to complement the overall color scheme of the room. In order to clean that ceiling, a special track was installed about a foot and a half from where the wall joins the ceiling. The track, although barely noticeable from the ground floor, enables workmen to hang a scaffold from it to simplify the cleaning of ceiling, walls, and mirrors.

(RIGHT)
Donald Deskey's Music Hall interiors brought him such fame he was urged to endorse new products. In this 1933 magazine advertisement he extolls the merits of Bakelite. (Courtesy of the library, Donald Deskey Archive, Cooper-Hewitt Museum: Smithsonian Institution.)

(FAR RIGHT)
Partial view of the Music Hall's Grand Lounge. (Herbert Gehr, Life Magazine © 1942, Time, Inc.)

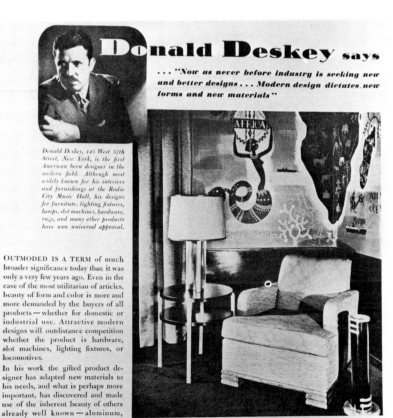

On the south wall of the Grand Foyer is a wide, railed balcony that extends from the promenade of the First Mezzanine for a view overlooking the entire room. Perhaps the most singularly eye-catching area of the foyer is the northern wall. A graceful grand staircase sweeps down from the First Mezzanine level, with a giant mural in muted tones dominating the wall above it. The staircase is covered with the same rust-colored patterned carpeting as the main floor, and blends with the Numidian marble on its side walls. But this staircase bears little resemblance to those that dominated earlier rococo movie palaces. Its softly sleek bronze and nickel bronze railing makes it look more like the elegant entranceway into the sunken salon of an enormous luxury liner.

Ezra Winter painted the mural that looms high above the first landing of the grand staircase. The mural, sixty feet wide and thirty feet high, was too big to paint inside a studio. Winter was forced to paint it on an unoccupied tennis court. Rendered in the basic colors of brick red, buff, and white, the painting helps establish a golden brown as the dominant color of the entire room. Winter's mural is based on an Oregon Indian legend that depicts the human race in its search for the fountain of youth and other unattainable ambitions and vanities. The great mountaintop, painted in a golden light, represents the impossible dream separated from the old man in the foreground of the painting by a chasm he cannot cross.

Staircases, in the same design as the one in the Grand Foyer, descend from either end of the huge room into the Grand Lounge. Deskey's feel for understated *moderne* elegance is well-displayed here. The room is stunning. The Grand Lounge is also large—two hundred feet long and eighty feet

wide—but it projects a feeling of seductive intimacy. The room was designed as a comfortable center for the patrons' relaxation between the acts and Deskey approached it as he did the private Rockefeller and Gimbel projects.

Soft indirect lighting sets the tone. The ceiling is relatively low and studded with diamond-shaped recessed lights. The shape of the lights is also carried out in a series of gleaming columns that divide the big room and minimize its size. These diamond-shaped piers are covered with black Carrara glass held in place by borders of bronze. Deskey designed the modern plaid carpet of gray, black, and rust. His furniture, chairs, tables, and couches dot the area, looking surprisingly contemporary considering their age.

The walls of the lounge are of black permatex, unadorned save for a series of subdued murals depicting scenes from various eras of the theater. The murals were painted by Louis Bouche. In keeping with his ideal of utilizing unusual materials, Deskey commissioned three different sculptors to create statues out of cast aluminum. "The Dancing Girl," by William Zorach, has a prominent place in the lounge where it guards the entranceway to the washrooms. Gwen Lux's "Eve" is on display off the Grand Foyer, and "The Girl and the Goose," by Robert Laurent, is positioned on the First Mezzanine. Deskey, operating on a tight budget, paid each artist a maximum of $1,500, and the statues were reportedly cast free of charge by the Aluminum Corporation.

Those three nudes became a cause célèbre before the Music Hall opened. Whether Roxy was completely serious or merely exercising his fine ear for free publicity has never been determined; nonetheless, he ordered the statues banned shortly before the opening. All the newspapers picked up the story that the great showman felt nude statues in his theater would be an insult to the proper morality of his patrons. In the end, RKO President Aylesworth overruled his director general and ordered them back into the theater. But only one, "The Girl and the Goose," made it in time for the opening night.

The ladies' room, off the Grand Lounge, features a fascinating mural by Witold Gordon entitled "History of Cosmetics." Gordon also designed the center rug. Here Deskey went all out in his use of special materials, covering the walls with white parchment. The furniture is constructed of sycamore and white lacquer and upholstered in a variety of fabrics including white kid, green damask, a high-pile beige, and a rough-textured rose.

Deskey pioneered the use of cork as a wall covering in the men's room off the Grand Lounge. He filled the room with aluminum-framed furniture (of his own design) covered in pigskin and plain linen. The floor is terrazzo and the copper-leafed ceiling blends with the copper light fixtures. A huge abstract painting by Stuart Davis entitled "Men Without Women" dominated the smoking room of the men's lounge. The painting is one of the few works of art not in their original positions at the Music Hall, having been donated in 1975 to New York's Museum of Modern Art. Davis became recognized as one of America's most important twentieth-century artists and the management felt the painting might be vandalized in the Music Hall.

The Music Hall is also one of the few theaters of its era to be equipped with banks of elevators for those patrons who were incapable or unwilling to traipse up the grand staircase. The elevators can whisk passengers from the basement lounge all the way up to the Third Mezzanine. They, too, are unique in design. The walls are highly polished bird's-eye maple with the beautiful hardwood inlays of American artist Edward Trumbull as a focal point.

Near the elevators at the north end of the Grand Lounge is a fully equipped doctor's office for any patrons needing emergency treatment.

Deskey designed the staggering total of thirty-one rest rooms throughout the Music Hall. In addition to having some 145 sinks for the paying customers, the lounges also offer some of the most in-

Deskey furniture against a Louis Bouche mural in the Grand Lounge. (Courtesy of the library, Donald Deskey Archive, Cooper-Hewitt Museum: Smithsonian Institution.)

The clean lines of Deskey-designed pieces in one of the Music Hall's many ladies' lounges. (Courtesy of the library, Donald Deskey Archive, Cooper-Hewitt Museum: Smithsonian Institution.)

teresting artwork in the theater. Rest rooms and smoking areas are available on every level of the Music Hall except off the Grand Foyer.

In a sense, the men's smoking rooms and women's powder rooms on the various levels of the building could be called mini-galleries. Each has appropriate murals by Gordon, Davis, Deskey, Kuniyoshi, Edward Buk Ulreich, and Henry Billings. Each of the rooms has its own character and theme because of Deskey's use of a variety of fabrics and materials that he considered appropriately masculine or feminine. Every detail is painstakingly integrated into the total composition.

The ladies' room on the Second Mezzanine is an especially beautiful example of Art Deco harmony. The walls are covered with huge green leaves and other flora in a mural painted by Yasuo Kuniyoshi. The outsized painted foliage is brought into proper perspective by the simple lines of Deskey's furniture, lamps, ashtrays, and mirrors.

One of the smaller women's powder rooms is made to look much more commodious by the use of mirrors. The room is polygonal-shaped with mirrors running up each wall from makeup table to ceiling. A nearby men's smoking room has a Deskey-designed mural depicting the history of tobacco. Perhaps the most interesting thing about this particular mural is that it is rendered on aluminum foil, manufactured by the R. J. Reynolds Tobacco Company.

One of the most opulent areas of the Music Hall has been seen by relatively few people over the years. Roxy insisted that the architects draw in plans for his own studio or mini-apartment on the eighth

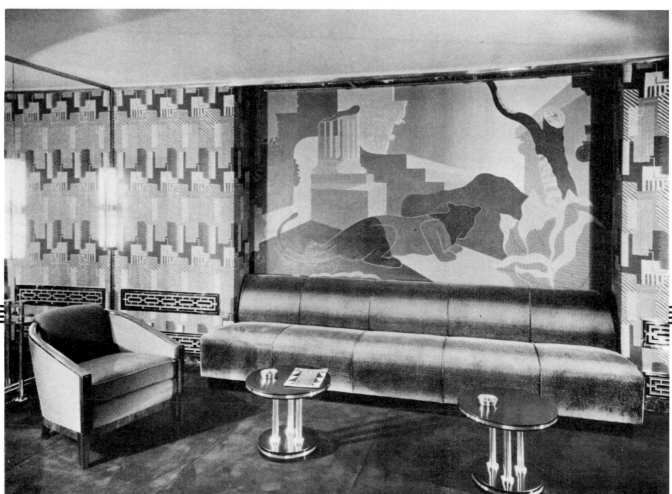

Witold Gordon's mural "Maps of the World" dominates the smoking room of the men's lounge on the First Mezzanine. His fondness for aluminum, Bakelite, walnut, and leather is apparent in Deskey's furniture for this room. (Courtesy of the library, Donald Deskey Archive, Cooper-Hewitt Museum: Smithsonian Institution.)

floor on the Fiftieth Street side of the building. It was an entirely livable area with a good-sized reception room, a round dining room, pantry, kitchen, and bathroom. Deskey, harking back to his pre-Music Hall career, designed a living area that displays the understated elegance of an imaginary apartment in a Gable-Harlow film of the 1930s. In later years, much of the area was altered into executive office space, although parts of it are still used for entertaining visiting dignitaries.

Deskey proved to be an excellent businessman as well as a brilliant designer. He had deliberately submitted a low estimate when he won the competition, and he worked wonders in creating a design masterpiece for something in the neighborhood of fifty thousand dollars. Of course, this was hardly pin money, but considering the way his contributions have stood the test of time, the sum seems paltry today. Deskey had commissioned the best artists he could find, and had supervised the interior decoration of the entire theater in addition to contributing many of his own works. And he had pulled it all together in less than a year!

It would take many hours to examine closely the detail of the artistry on display at the Radio City Music Hall. Deskey's pleasingly voluptuous chairs and couches are scattered about on the promenades of the mezzanines and lounges as are his Bakelite and aluminum tables and round mirrors. Little unexpected wonders are everywhere. It is easy to overlook art objects like the bronze relief scenes of theatrical life that grace the stainless-steel doors leading into the auditorium.

In their closed-door meetings following the opening, the Radio City management had to face some facts. Was it impossible, as critic Brooks Atkinson had said, that variety show performers were

(TOP) Informal lounge grouping of overstuffed furniture designed by Donald Deskey for the Music Hall. (Courtesy of the library, Donald Deskey Archive, Cooper-Hewitt Museum: Smithsonian Institution.)

(BOTTOM) Henry Billings' mural of a crouching panther forms a backdrop for Deskey's comfortably simple pieces in the women's powder room on the Third Mezzanine. (Courtesy of the library, Donald Deskey Archive, Cooper-Hewitt Museum: Smithsonian Institution.)

The men's smoking room on the Second Mezzanine is all Deskey. Furniture of his design sits before his own mural "Nicotine," which depicts the growth of tobacco from field to cigar. Deskey persuaded the American Tobacco Company to donate the aluminum foil on which the mural is rendered. (Courtesy of the library, Donald Deskey Archive, Cooper-Hewitt Museum: Smithsonian Institution.)

Deskey's love for elegant simplicity is demonstrated in this upholstered bench of his design. Identical benches are scattered throughout the Music Hall's public corridors. (Courtesy of the library, Donald Deskey Archive, Cooper-Hewitt Museum: Smithsonian Institution.)

"lost" on the Music Hall stage? Had Roxy wildly miscalculated in his belief that spectacular variety shows were the perfect entertainment for an auditorium and stage that had been built to his own specifications?

To some of the assembled executives the idea seemed almost blasphemous. After all, Roxy was the *master showman;* his theatrical genius had never been questioned. That is why they had hired him and given him carte blanche. His judgment had been infallible, with nothing to mar his record . . . until December 27, 1932. Businessmen, like chefs, have reason to believe "the proof is in the pudding." The pudding, in this instance, was the file of box office receipts balanced against the staggering outlay of cash advanced for the opening production. (Two weeks after its opening, the Music Hall would have a two-hundred-thousand-dollar operating deficit.)

There was no time to lose. The Music Hall Board of Directors felt that drastic measures were called for immediately. In a very short period of time a series of directives were issued that would completely alter the long-planned course of the new theater. Leon Leonidoff had been with Roxy for years. It was thought that he knew all of his mentor's "theatrical tricks" and would be able to fill in for him until Roxy was able to return. In the future the stage shows would be no longer than fifty minutes in length. Never again would outrageous salaries be paid to big-name stars.

Most importantly, the Radio City Music Hall *would* begin to include feature motion pictures as part of the overall program, starting with the new production, which would open January 11, 1933. The new bill would feature the film *The Bitter Tea of General Yen,* starring Nils Asther and Barbara Stanwyck, *plus* a live show on the Great Stage. Roxy, in the hospital, was unable to condone or condemn the decision. Ironically, it was the same format he had made famous . . . and vice versa.

FOUR

THE HOUSE
THAT ROXY BUILT

With the official announcement of a sweeping change in format at the Music Hall, there was an immediate spate of column notes and teasing articles in the newspapers reporting that Roxy was "out" at the theater he had helped create. The Music Hall management refused to comment on the reports and Roxy was unable to do so. He had been isolated in his hospital room by his doctor's orders.

It was a natural (if not accurate) conclusion for the reporters to reach. Roxy's spectacular show had been a failure and his theater was continuing on without him, utilizing an entertainment policy he had publicly derided as "old hat" long before his illness. Many members of the press publicly sided with the Music Hall management in its decision to bring in the new movie–stage show policy. They, along with some of his associates, considered Roxy's first failure a direct result of his own attempt to go "high hat." They reasoned that only excessive and misguided self-indulgence would cause him to desert a policy that had proved so successful.

Whatever his feeling after the Music Hall had made its decision to change format without consulting him, there is strong documentation that before his illness he was adamantly opposed to movies at the Music Hall. On the surface, that stance did seem strange for a man who had risen to the top of his profession through his imaginative handling of motion-picture presentation. But a close study of Rothafel's life and work reveals that this sometimes-brash, self-educated man had the soul of an artist. Constantly striving for perfection, he was never content to live on past glories. His public utterances disclose his healthy respect for the audience long before he came to the Music Hall. He was intent on giving them the most aesthetically satisfying and entertaining shows his budget could provide. He was adamantly opposed to following trends or previously established popular ideas. His own instincts would, he thought, tell him what would uplift and entertain rather than the still-popular, short-sighted dictum of "Give 'em what they want!"

Before the Music Hall opening, Roxy was asked by a reporter what he planned to do at the new theater. He replied: "Everything you could possibly imagine. We believe the public wants better things than most theatrical managers think. The great trouble with our amusements has been that the producers have been pandering instead of catering to the public tastes."

It was S. L. Rothafel, more than any other showman of his time, who had introduced the masses of ordinary American people to great music, symphonic and operatic, as well as to ballet and other forms of dance. And those who had come only to see a popular "show" had generally found themselves in for an agreeable surprise. That first opening night at the Music Hall was the exception to the rule. There had been too much of everything.

Roxy's hospital stay, following the operation, was a long one. When reporters were finally allowed to visit him, they found him a tired, sad man who had aged rapidly, but who refused to be bitter about the way his great theater had been changed in his absence. In a bedside interview with a reporter for the New York *Sun,* he said he was sure he would be called back to the Music Hall to continue the work that was so important to him. On his doctor's advice, he was going to Florida to soak up some sun and regain his health. He'd be back in April ready to get the Music Hall on an even keel again.

He did return about five months later to find his plans altered almost beyond recognition. Many of the people he hired had disappeared and new people had been brought in; Roxy himself had become just another employee. The handwriting was on the wall for Roxy to see. The new interim management headed by H. B. Franklin, president of the RKO Theatre Companies, had shown their further disdain for his talents by cutting his two-thousand-dollar-a-week salary in half. It was an entirely new situation and he became something of an outsider in the theater he had built.

He continued on as director general of the Music Hall through the remaining months of 1933 but only as a figurehead. He would tell intimates later that he was constantly being called to meetings with the three representatives of RKO and their three counterparts from Rockefeller Center who made up the Music Hall Board of Directors. He would listen to them argue various points, but was seldom asked to give an opinion, "as though I weren't even in the same room."

The rumors continued to fly that Roxy was on his way out of the Music Hall. Still he kept a cheerful public face. In a question-and-answer session with reporters he was asked if the Rockefeller interests had found him overly extravagant. His answer: "Can you imagine the Rockefellers building Radio City and calling me extravagant. Have a cigar? The only thing I did that might be called wasteful was to hire taxi cabs to go from one part of the Music Hall to another."

In answer to a question about any differences between himself and the management over his stage presentations, Roxy admitted there had been one difference, saying, "They wanted me to cut my ballet company by 10 percent, but I didn't want to embarrass Roosevelt by flooding the country with fifteen million unemployed."

Asked about the new policy of movies at the Music Hall, Roxy said, "I never pay any attention to pictures. Who are the most popular movie stars these days anyhow, Beverly Baine and William Farnum?" Asked if he had heard the rumor that Germany's famed Max Reinhardt was about to replace him, Roxy shook his head and said, "No, but he's a good man. It's a lovely world. Have a bottle of champagne!" In answer to a question concerning any possible bitterness he might feel about the situation at the Music Hall, Roxy said, "I am incapable of bitterness. I love everybody. I love the Radio City Chiefs, the big Whatzises. Have a piano?"

But as time went by his unaccustomed helplessness inside the mighty theater increased his frustration. Despite the production cutbacks, the Music Hall continued to lose money. His bargaining position was weakened further when the Seventh Avenue Roxy Theatre forced RKO to change the name of Radio Center's RKO Roxy theater at Forty-ninth Street and Sixth Avenue. The Music Hall's sister theater, the place where he had planned to satisfy the money men by showing films and popular entertainment, was abruptly renamed the Center Theatre. Unlike the Music Hall, the Center Theatre never had a continuous policy. It was variously used for movies, variety shows, legitimate plays, ice shows, etc. It fell to the wrecker's ball in 1954.

Roxy Rothafel's stormy association with the Music Hall came to an end early in 1934, little more than a year after the grand opening. Roxy found it more dignified to leave than to stay and endure the increasing numbers of restrictions placed upon him. He had never been a man who could live with restrictions. Admitting the long-rumored differences between himself and the management, he informed the press that he had finally tired of it all "and walked out on them." Radio City spokesmen would only say that Roxy "had exceeded his budget and resisted supervision."

Roxy insisted that 1933 had ended successfully, with a good run for the motion picture *Little Women*. He added, "I had to fight to get the committee to accept it." He insisted that he still felt no bitterness, but a farewell letter he wrote to the Music Hall projectionists said, "Had we been left alone and encouraged, it could have meant but one thing—unbounded success; but it was not to be." Later he sued the Music Hall for back salary owed him on what he considered a broken contract.

There was one more flurry of excitement in Roxy's career, when he attempted to save the Mastbaum Theatre in Philadelphia, but the times were not ripe and his best efforts were not enough. The Mastbaum closed within a few months and Roxy was left to brood over the reasons for still another failure. His health continued to decline as his spirits flagged.

Roxy was discovered dead in his bed on the morning of January 13, 1936, a little more than

RADIO · KEITH · ORPHEUM
PROUDLY PRESENTS
THE INAUGURAL PROGRAM
OF THE
RKO ROXY THEATRE
IN RADIO CITY
49th Street and 6th Avenue
UNDER THE PERSONAL DIRECTION OF

The smaller RKO Roxy Theatre, a block down Sixth Avenue from the Music Hall, opened with considerably less fanfare a few days later. In time its name would be changed to the Center Theater. (Courtesy of Earle Moss.)

three years after he had opened the Music Hall . . . just two years since he had left it forever. Jan Peerce chanted the Jewish Prayer for the Dead at his funeral and a squad from his beloved Marine Corps fired the traditional volleys over his grave. He was fifty-three years old.

Samuel Lionel "Roxy" Rothafel was a contemporary of another famous and flamboyant character named George Herman "Babe" Ruth. The great home-run hitter's influence was so powerful that Yankee Stadium became known as "The House That Ruth Built." Using the same logic, Rothafel's guidance and inspiration in the creation of Radio City Music Hall makes that great theater eligible for the title "The House That Roxy Built."

The late Ed Sullivan perhaps summed up Roxy's contribution best in his New York *Daily News* column of January 12, 1937. He wrote:

Which brings me to the anniversary of Roxy's death. I see by the papers there is a movement underfoot to erect a tablet to him . . . a tablet? . . . What about Radio City? . . . Could any man have a greater monument? Radio City came into existence through Roxy's genius as a promoter . . . I call it genius because it required that for any one person to sell the Rockefellers such a colossal idea as this group of buildings. If that were not sufficient, there is the Roxy Theatre named after him on Seventh Avenue. Wherever you go in the country you'll find other Roxy Theatres. . . . In Detroit I even found a shoeshine parlor with the named emblazoned across the dingy window. Probably he felt when he was released from Radio City that his life had been a failure. . . . But actually he was a great success. . . . To create Radio City was as significant in our generation as to have built the pyramids . . . and Radio City was built to add to the entertainment of this country. I don't think that Roxy needs a tablet because nothing can compare to what he erected in his lifetime. Anybody who pierces the hustle and bustle of this century and makes himself known, even for a brief moment, has done something worthwhile . . . or so it seems to me.

FIVE

LEONIDOFF: Master of the Spectacle

No single person has ever been selected to replace Roxy in the hierarchy at Radio City Music Hall. An obvious reason for this is Roxy's decision to create his own (entirely suitable) title: director general. Nobody since has been able to claim it.

More importantly, even before his official departure, the business end of the Music Hall had been handled by a committee . . . half RKO and half Rockefeller Center, Inc. When RKO folded, Rockefeller Center, Inc., went on alone as the financial interest with ultimate control of the Music Hall's destiny. To be sure, there have been a succession of Music Hall presidents and executive vice-presidents who seemingly called the shots from the public point of view. But there was usually a more powerful Rockefeller Center, Inc., president looking over their collective shoulders. No one man or woman has since wielded Roxy's monumental influence over the entire operation of the great New York theater.

On the purely creative side, a number of people have been responsible for the overall production during the past five decades. The names Leon Leonidoff, Russell Markert, Marc Platt, John Jackson, and Peter Gennaro have been most enduring. Of these five, Leonidoff and Markert are far and away the most important, with Leonidoff the more prolific of these two.

Leonidoff came to America as a tiny bundle of ballet-dancing energy early in the century. He quickly discovered that Americans were not so interested in the European dance form as his native Romanians. He was eager to learn the peculiar artistic customs of his adopted land, and over a period of time found perhaps the ideal teacher. In the 1920s he met Roxy, who quickly took a fancy to the young Romanian immigrant. Roxy would question him for hours on his opinions of theater as it was practiced in Europe. In time, Leonidoff was signed on as an assistant to this man who headed the artistic endeavors at the Capitol Theatre.

For whatever reasons, Leonidoff seldom mentions these early days of his career. But many of his contemporaries say he started as little more than Roxy's "gopher," a young man willing to run errands for his mentor. If that was truly the case, the apprentice learned his lessons well. By the time Roxy opened the Roxy Theatre on Seventh Avenue, Leonidoff was an imaginative and trusted aide of the Master. In the opening Music Hall program he was billed as production director. When Roxy's illness pulled him away after the opening night, it was Leonidoff who took over the supervision of the stage productions. He continued in the capacity of senior producer until he left the Music Hall in 1974.

In the spring of 1978, still feisty and imaginative in his eighties, Leonidoff told a network television audience that he started working with Roxy and designer Peter Clark on ideas for the Music Hall stage in February of 1930. That was almost a year before either Roxy or he had announced their resignations from the Roxy Theatre. Whatever his personal contributions to the original design of the stage and all its components, his use of it through nearly forty-two years at the Music Hall proved that he understood it like no other person.

What Leonidoff inherited at the Music Hall when Roxy left has been described, in elegant simplicity, as "the most perfectly equipped stage in the world." That statement is generally conceded to be as true today as it was in 1932. Only a professional could be expected to understand and appreciate fully all the facets of that great stage, but a rundown of its vital statistics should be of interest to any layperson who has ever seen so much as one stage production anywhere.

Remember the great movie musicals of the 1940s and 1950s? Fred Astaire and Ginger Rogers or Gene Kelly and Cyd Charisse and others were forever portraying dancers on the Broadway stage. The climactic scene usually showed the loving duo finding true romance and proving the validity of their artistic struggle by performing a spectacular dance, amid clouds of smoke and other effects, on a stage that seemingly stretched from Culver City to Times Square. Since actual Broadway stages have never been that vast or that well-equipped, perhaps those film-makers had the Radio City stage in mind when they envisioned a legitimate stage. The Music Hall stage can literally re-create, before a live audience, almost any wild idea Hollywood's technology can devise on a sound stage.

First of all, consider the size of the stage. It measures 144 feet wide and 66½ feet deep. If Gene Kelly were standing in the stage right wings looking at Vera Ellen in the wings on stage left, he might have to use binoculars. They would be nearly a city block apart. The total proscenium opening is larger than that of any theater anywhere.

The special effects are even more spectacular. Consider this: When a Music Hall director wants a scene performed in a rainstorm, he simply instructs his stage manager to cue the lowering of a special "rain curtain" and the stage is filled with a spray of real water. In reality, the rain "curtain" consists of two long pipes suspended in the fly gallery high over the stage. The pipes have a series of holes drilled into their undersides and are connected to a water source on the stage. When water is pumped into them, a steady stream of "rain" falls down onto the stage. When the rain effect is used, the first stage elevator is covered with a waterproof canvas. At the conclusion of the show, the elevator is lowered five inches, causing the canvas to form a trough. The water floods into the trough and thence into a hose where it is carried away.

If fog, clouds, and less drastic forms of moisture are called for in a scene, a special "steam curtain" supplies this effect. The steam is the natural stuff, supplied by the city of New York. A metal plate, with a series of closely spaced holes in it, runs along the full width of the stage floor. City steam is pressurized and forced up through the holes on command, forming a veritable curtain of steam. This device is always used at the very end of the finale so the stage won't be too slippery for dancing and other

Leon Leonidoff at his director's table in the orchestra seats of the Music Hall during a dress rehearsal in the 1940s. (Herbert Gehr, Life Magazine © 1942, Time, Inc.)

A rare glimpse of the bare Music Hall stage. (Courtesy of Bob Coogan.)

Backstage workers, standing at stage level in the foreground, look down on two of the stage floor elevators that have been lowered to the scenery docks fourteen feet below. (Courtesy of Bob Coogan.)

movement. Leonidoff introduced another special curtain, which gives the lifelike electrical effect of a full-scale fireworks display.

From a purely technical point of view, the most impressive devices on the stage are the elevators. In essence, a great area of the vast stage is entirely movable. From close to the main curtain line in front and not too distant from the back wall in depth, nearly half of the total 144-foot width of the stage is the flooring of three elevators. Each elevator, comprising that area of the stage floor to a width of 70 feet, can be raised to a height some 13 feet above the normal stage floor or lowered, in one piece or in three sections, all the way to subbasement level. In other words, if the director wants to create a "mountain" on his stage, he can do so with the use of the elevators. By the same token, he can create a mighty chasm or move his performers and/or sets up and down at will.

These three stage elevators, along with the special orchestra carriage, weigh a total of 190 tons and are considered the most innovative use of immense moving platforms this side of the U.S. Navy's aircraft carrier elevators. In fact, there is a Music Hall story that government agents were present at all times during World War II to prevent enemy agents from examining the elevators with the intent of stealing the theory for possible military application.

Inside the perimeter of the elevators is a huge turntable that can be used for quick scene changes or special stage effects. The turntable can also be lowered to subbasement level or raised to an area thirteen feet above the normal stage floor.

Included in the collection of massive stage machinery is a device the technical directors refer to as the "orchestra bandwagon." It is an apt coinage to describe one of the most breathtaking effects in the Music Hall. A modern-day spectator is not particularly surprised to see an orchestra rise mysteriously from nowhere to its place in the orchestra pit at the front edge of the stage. But what if that full symphony orchestra doesn't stop at the orchestra pit level? What if it rises to stage level and then proceeds (tootling merrily) to move majestically backward, under its own power, all the way to the rear of the stage where it suddenly sinks out of sight? The Music Hall Symphony Orchestra can also be playing in its pit at the front of the stage, disappear and within seconds rise magically into view at the extreme rear of the stage.

The Music Hall stage has often been called the perfect stage for dancers, but the steel tracks and bolsters for the elevators, turntable, and bandwagon can also pose a hazard. Rockettes and Ballet Company members must be constantly aware of the subtly raised metal edges of these devices that crisscross the playing area.

As might be expected, the Radio City Music Hall is equipped with a mind-boggling number of lights. In fact, in one of its early press releases before energy conservation became a priority, the Music Hall boasted its lighting system used enough power each year to supply the electrical needs of a city of ten thousand people. In 1978 the publicity department took the more conservative approach that "if every bulb in the Music Hall was burning at the same time, over three million watts would be in use." Concentrating only on those light bulbs of varying size that directly affect the stage production, there are some 1,950 on the stage, 500 used for a star effect on stage, and 7,184 used in the auditorium.

Roxy and his original Music Hall associates were not the first to place a light console in the auditorium of a theater, but they did perfect the innovation. The Music Hall's light control console was manufactured by the General Electric Company and is fifteen and a half feet long, three and a half feet wide, and five and a half feet high. The console device occupies a space out of the audience's vision directly in front of the first row of orchestra seats. The master electrician who controls it sits in front of a keyboard containing 4,305 color-keyed handles, that can flood the stage with a variety of lighting effects. These individual handles can be preset before a show and then operated during the performance by a master switch and dimmer that can come up with twenty different combinations.

This marvel of technology operates on the principle of the radio tube. Because of its thermionic control system, it is from six to eight times smaller than other light boards capable of handling an equal number of controls. It is also equipped with a selsyn automatic color change control that does away with the need for an individual lighting man to hand-change the metal gelatin holders in front of each spotlight. The gelatins provide the stage with colored lighting effects. The selsyn-equipped spotlights have a metal housing containing four colored gelatins that move across the front of the light on tiny tracks, powered by small motors. All of these lights can be operated by one individual sitting at the console. Music Hall arc lamps are also equipped with electrically operated "blackout dousers," metal shutters that close over the face of the lamp in two seconds. Normally, arc lamps will continue to give off a faint glow for up to half a minute after they're turned off. With the automatic dousers, the Music Hall stage is totally dark at the immediate conclusion of a "blackout scene."

Lighting is one of the most important components in any stage production, and the Music Hall is equipped with a dazzling array of lighting paraphernalia that can be remotely operated by the central console in front of the stage. The original stage equipment includes six 104-foot light bridges (the largest ever built), which hold literally hundreds of spotlights of different sizes to bathe the stage in brilliance. The auditorium console also controls six light towers holding lights capable of putting out nearly ten thousand watts of spot and flood power each.

When even bigger spotlights are needed, they are manned by individual people in two separate booths at the very top of the back wall of the vast auditorium on either side of the projection room. These mammoth 150-ampere spots are used to wash special areas of the stage in extra-brilliant light, or to "follow" individual singers or dancers. The light booths are also equipped with Linnebach Lanterns capable of projecting lifelike outdoor scenes on a specially constructed screen on the stage, creating still another dimension for the patron's imagination. High above the heads of the audience in the curved ceiling is a special light cove equipped with six more 150-ampere arc lights.

There is also a hand-controlled lighting switchboard backstage. This board operates the footlights on the stage apron (which can be automatically raised or lowered flush with the stage floor) as well as the footlights for the great curved cyclorama at the rear of the stage. The lights that flood the cyclorama curtain can create a feeling of infinite space for dazzling sunrises, sunsets, and any number of other natural-looking effects. The stage light board also controls the ceiling lights that bathe the audience in overhead color. Inside the semicircular, fluted bands in the ceiling are three thousand reflectors in eight strips, capable of painting the ceiling in brilliant or muted color.

It has been reported that Roxy ordered some last-minute alterations inside the Music Hall auditorium scant hours before the opening curtain in 1932. He was concerned about the acoustics in the vast hall, which contains over 1,800,000 cubic feet of space. Even his acoustical plaster "megaphone" design couldn't completely correct the problem. Today, Broadway shows in theaters of less than one thousand seats use microphones and intricate sound systems to pick up the singing and speaking voices of performers who have, presumably, been trained in the art of stage projection.

The Music Hall was one of the earliest users of an amplification system because of the size of its auditorium. RCA called in its finest engineers to design and build the largest master control console ever constructed. Today the Music Hall has a high fidelity sound reproduction system that is completely stereophonic, with the sound coming from speakers directly in front of the stage performers. The stage microphones are hidden along the front of the stage and rise into position automatically at the press of a button.

Radio City ballerinas, on the second level, look down at the giant elevator pistons, which have raised their platforms to stage level high above them. (Herbert Gehr, Life Magazine © 1942, Time, Inc.)

Leonidoff's apprenticeship under Roxy served him well. He was determined to use the equipment with such extravagance and prolificacy that he would become the rightful inheritor of Roxy's mantle as "Master of the Spectacle." It is interesting to note that the Music Hall's producers have never fully exploited all the special stage machinery since Leonidoff's departure in 1974. During his tenure at the world's greatest theater, he filled its stages with animals at the Christmas Pageant, medieval cathedrals at Eastertime, rockets during the heyday of televised NASA lift-offs, jet planes, trains, automobiles, and all other manner of immense objects never seen on a stage.

The fiery little producer was never a man to settle for smallness in anything—except for his own physical stature, which he was powerless to change. As an example, for many years he kept a luxurious apartment in New York's Waldorf Towers. He felt his son should have a room suitable for a growing boy-child, so he talked the great Walt Disney into personally supervising the design and decoration of the boy's private chamber.

Leonidoff knew the workings of the Great Stage better than any living man. He had a mania for utilizing every bit of the equipment and would not hesitate to rent other gadgets if the Music Hall didn't already possess them. In one show, with a Roman theme, he decided to stage a chariot race. Instead of asking the art department what they could come up with in effects for the race, he imported treadmills, three real chariots, and six *live* horses. He instructed the drivers to gallop the horses madly along on the treadmills, and the result was as spectacular as he had planned.

Leonidoff also has specific ideas about the kind of performers he believed best for the Music Hall. About to embark on one of his numerous European talent hunts he told reporters, "It's essential we have a certain type of act—acrobats, knock-about comics, circus style acts—because our stage is so big that you can't fill it with talk. The effect must be spectacularly visual."

Whether true or not, the longtime employees at the Music Hall still chuckle at a story they attribute to Leonidoff. The Christmas and Easter pageants, thanks to Leon, have been a Music Hall tradition

The Music Hall's intricate light console is tucked away from the view of the audience at the front of the stage apron in the huge auditorium. (Herbert Gehr, Life Magazine © 1942, Time, Inc.)

In a view never seen by the audience, the powerful beams of the spotlights from the lighting booths high on the back wall of the auditorium pick out the Rockettes facing upstage. (Courtesy of Cosmo-Sileo Associates.)

from the beginning. One year he decided to add something new to make the Easter show even bigger. He wanted to stage a tableau depicting the Last Supper. All went well until the first rehearsal when Leon started to block out the scene. He studied the stage for a long moment and his face turned a fiery red.

"No, no, no, no!" he bellowed. "It's all wrong! What have you done to my Last Supper? The stage is empty. There must be more people at that table!"

He scratched the tableau when somebody quietly explained to him, in the interest of historical accuracy, that no more than twelve people could be allowed at the table for the Last Supper.

By the same token, his thick Romanian accent also sometimes confused his underlings, as on the occasion when he demanded a "dingdong, like *Ivan* calling!" He finally got his bell, but the *Avon* Company got no apology. On another occasion, he startled all the participants at a dress rehearsal by jumping to his feet and screaming, "Where are the whales?" Panic ensued until someone realized he was inquiring about the *veils,* missing from the costumes of the dancing girls.

Leonidoff was a charmer who delighted in calling nearly everyone "Dolling!" when things were going well. But, according to longtime associates, he could be a stern taskmaster when his authority was challenged. They tell of a member of the backstage staff who had a heated encounter with the senior producer and was fired on the spot. According to the story, Leonidoff relented the next day and hired the man back once he had agreed to make a formal apology in front of the entire company.

Leonidoff's flaming temperament brought on some legendary feuds with his Music Hall associates. One veteran swears that another associate once punched Leon to the floor. Leonidoff's head reportedly hit a radiator on the way down, rendering him unconscious. He says further that a backstage worker threw a telephone at him, and an esteemed member of the music department once had to be physically restrained from hurling himself at the producer during one of their famed shouting matches.

In many ways, Leonidoff was very much like his mentor, Roxy. He was, during his Music Hall days, a man of flamboyant personality and strong will, who was capable of extreme acts of kindness. Like Roxy, he had his own factotum in the person of Nicholas Daks, whose job it was to act as buffer and all-around assistant. Once Leonidoff believed in a performer or craftsman, his loyalty was unswerving.

His judgment was not unimpeachable. Metropolitan Opera star Leonard Warren, like his counterparts Jan Peerce and Robert Weede, was once a member of the Radio City Chorus. He was young and grateful for the steady work, but he desperately wanted an opportunity to prove himself as a soloist. Leonidoff already had his featured soloist, a man who had been with him for some time. Every time Warren would plead with the producer to give him a chance to take the spotlight, Leonidoff would tell him he was an expert chorus singer but had no chance of ever becoming a soloist as good as the one he was using.

But his detractors at the Music Hall all agree that things have never been the same since Leon left. They say he used all the equipment on the stage like nobody else and seemed to have an uncanny sense of what the audience wanted.

Although he left the Music Hall in 1974, retirement has never been an easy way of life for the ebullient Leonidoff. His years of world travel in search of new acts to add to his Music Hall spectaculars have left him restless and eager to continue. As recently as the spring of 1978, he was talking to his confidants about plans for producing gorgeous new shows at the big casino-hotels scheduled to open in Atlantic City, New Jersey. His only fear . . . would the stages be big enough to hold his kind of show!

SIX

The Rocket Man

For close to forty years Russell Markert alternated with Leon Leonidoff in producing the mammoth stage shows at the Radio City Music Hall. In later years, they would take turns staging even the most traditional shows such as those at Christmas and Easter. Each was sent on trips to various parts of the world to scout new specialty acts for upcoming productions. Today Music Hall veterans seem divided on the subject of which man was more talented.

One comment from an old-timer seems a fair summary: "Leon was probably more commercial. He seemed to have a greater appeal for the masses. Russell's shows were more sophisticated. He concentrated on the performances and approached the whole thing more like a Ziegfeld."

Even if Russell Markert had been the greatest producer in history, that part of his career would always be overshadowed by just one special contribution among his many theatrical credits: He was the creator and director of the Radio City Music Hall Rockettes.

Russell was a skinny, red-haired lad out of a Westfield, New Jersey, high school when he got his first real taste of show business . . . in France of all places, with the American Expeditionary Forces during World War I. As he tells it, he was something of the "company cutup" in the services and supplies branch of the army. After the Armistice was signed, he was stationed with the headquarters of his branch in Tours, France. YMCA representatives came around asking for volunteers to participate in an "all-doughboy" show. Even as a child, he had enjoyed hopping around to music, as he puts it, and had been a member of the boys choir at St. Stephen's Church in Jersey City. His army buddies prodded him into auditioning for the YMCA show and he got the job. That became the first tentative step in a career that carried him to the top of his profession.

After the war, he followed more practical advice and took a job on Wall Street while continuing his education in night school. A classmate provided an escape from the world of stocks and bonds by telling him that Earl Carroll was looking for college boys for his first *Vanities* in 1923. Russell, reasoning that night school attendance made him a legitimate college boy, auditioned and got the job on Broadway. With the steady income from his chorus role in the *Vanities,* he could afford to enroll in serious courses teaching all forms of dance. His professional career had been launched.

Markert also trained as a singer in those early years and his studies paid off when he was chosen as the juvenile lead in the second company of the smash hit *No, No, Nanette.* Unfortunately, the show wasn't ready to go on the road for seven or eight weeks and the producer wasn't ready to pay anyone or sign a contract until rehearsals began. Markert's agent, Sammy Lee, fretted about his talented client's lack of income and asked Russell to join him for lunch at the Lambs Club. Lee wanted him to meet two important people who could give him immediate, paying employment if he was interested.

The agent's friends turned out to be the Skouras brothers, Spyros and Charles, who would later climb to the highest echelons of Hollywood moguldom. The brothers had recently taken over the three-thousand-seat Missouri Theatre in St. Louis and were looking around for someone to produce the stage shows for them. They liked what they saw in the dapper young man with the red hair. The offer of an immediate livelihood was tempting, even though his proposed salary would be considerably less than he had been promised for *No, No, Nanette.*

"I had seen the John Tiller Girls in the *Ziegfeld Follies* of 1922," he says. "And I thought to myself, if I can ever get a chance to get a group of American girls who would be taller and have longer legs, and could do really complicated tap routines and eye-high kicks instead of just simple buck and wings and little waist-high kicks . . . that would be one of the things I'd really want to do sometime in the future."

So he went home that night to Westfield with the assurance that he had two jobs in the offing. One more satisfying to his ego that would pay him more money when it started; the other, immediate money and a chance to go into another area of the business where he could fulfil one of his long-term dreams. He flipped a quarter; it came out St. Louis, and the group that was to become the world-famous Rockettes was born.

When they made their formal debut in St. Louis in 1925, Markert officially billed them as the Missouri Rockets. He was pleased to find St. Louis a cultural oasis on the Mississippi in the mid-1920s, and was able to sign sixteen excellent dancers out of the many he auditioned. Markert's producing efforts at the Missouri Theatre were highly successful, and his "Rockets" were a smash hit. Within months their fame had grown and they were ready to take to the road.

The Skouras brothers became involved in a chain of showcase houses known as the Publix Theatres and encouraged Russell to take his Rockets to Atlanta, Buffalo, Detroit, Kansas City, and many other places including Chicago. In the Windy City he expanded the group, renamed them "The Sixteen American Rockets," and played two Balaban and Katz theaters at the same time. New York City, the Big Apple, was next. He took the Rockets into the Rivoli Theatre and they became an immediate sensation. He was flooded with all kinds of offers.

Markert decided the best of the offers was one for a tour with the "Greenwich Village Follies," produced by Jones and Green. It was a tremendously popular revue in those days and Markert decided, once and for all, that he had got the lucky turn when he flipped the quarter back in Westfield, New Jersey, across the Hudson. The troupe had a successful tour and returned to New York for a Broadway show called *Rain or Shine,* with Joe Cooke and Tom Howard. Two other members of that cast were Warren Hull, who later went on to fame as a master of ceremonies on radio and television, and Dave Chasen, who left the performing end of show business to open one of Hollywood's most celebrity-studded restaurants. Markert was hired to do all the choreography for the show in addition to bringing in his Rockets dance line as a special feature.

They were setting the routines for *Rain or Shine* at the old Bryant rehearsal hall in downtown Manhattan when a chance meeting altered the course of American dance history. Conductor Charles Previn, whom Markert had worked with in St. Louis, decided to pay him a visit at the rehearsal hall. Previn suggested to his current boss, S. L. Rothafel, that he accompany him on the visit to see a "really remarkable group of girl dancers." In late 1927 Roxy went to the Bryant rehearsal, saw the Rockets, and a show business saga was born.

Roxy, who had recently opened the theater that carried his name, was tremendously impressed with the Rockets and wanted to hire them on the spot for his new "Cathedral of the Motion Picture." Markert explained that he was already tied up with a "book show," but Roxy wouldn't accept the refusal. He insisted that he absolutely must have the Rockets in the Roxy cast, and suggested that they work in his show until they were ready to do *Rain or Shine.* Markert accepted.

The Rockets were so much of an instant hit at the Roxy Theatre, Rothafel was loathe to let them leave when the time came to honor their previous commitment for the Broadway show. He pleaded with Markert to form another line to replace the departing Rockets. With the aid of a friend, Markert rounded up another sixteen excellent dancers, trained them and choreographed their routines, and found himself with two lines of Rockets. One group of sixteen Rockets was working in a Broadway show and the other at the Roxy Theatre. With both troupes going strong, Markert scouted out more dancers and formed a third Rocket company, which worked in vaudeville on the "Subway Circuit," a number of outlying theaters in the Greater New York Metropolitan area.

Markert's line of sixteen dancing girls grew in size because of a sudden Roxy inspiration. The great showman was so impressed with the Rockets that he approached Markert with an idea. Why not bring the two groups of Rockets into the Roxy Theatre to work together for the Easter show? Markert liked the idea and introduced the two troupes in separate numbers on the Roxy stage, bringing them together in a line of thirty-two girls for the high-kicking finale. Thirty-two became a permanent group at the Roxy, being renamed the "Roxyettes." Russell says today he approved of the idea, although he and Roxy never had any written contract between them.

When Roxy announced his new affiliation with the Radio City Music Hall, Russell Markert and the Roxyettes were a prime part of the package. Although Brooks Atkinson made only a sidelong note of them in his opening review, they were and are an integral part of every Music Hall production. Perhaps because of the legal name troubles with the Roxy Theatre, Markert decided to change the name of the Music Hall Roxyettes back to their original name. They had become known as the Rockets all across America before they joined the Roxy Theatre company. Markert decided he could make the name more feminine by adding another *t* and an *e*. The most famous precision dance team in the world would thereafter be known as the Rockettes.

During the late 1920s and early 1930s, Markert had as many as ninety-six girls working for him in various shows in New York. Sixteen of his girls were in the Marx Brothers' vehicle *Animal Crackers*

Old friend Lucille Ball and her then husband, Desi Arnaz, pay a visit to Markert and his Rockettes at the Music Hall during the early 1950s. (Courtesy of Cosmo-Sileo Associates.)

as a special group, and he also did choreography for two of George White's *Scandals* productions—"Picking Cotton" and "The Black Bottom." He also produced the first "Ice Capades," "Roller Skating Vanities," and "Holiday on Ice." In 1929 he took sixteen of his best dancing girls in a special railroad car to Hollywood for an appearance in the *King of Jazz,* a musical film starring Paul Whiteman, among others.

In 1934 Markert was asked to do the choreography for a new film called *Moulin Rouge,* starring Constance Bennett and Franchot Tone. Again, he took some of his favorite dancers with him. It was on this film that he met his lifelong friend, Lucille Ball. At the time they were reported to be having a torrid romance, and though it never blossomed into marriage, the friendship still flourishes. In fact, Lucy met her present husband, Gary Morton, while he was doing a stand-up comedy act at the Music Hall.

Wherever Russell Markert wandered, he always returned to his beloved Rockettes. He says today he never deliberately set out to choose a line of "All-American Beauties"—it just seemed to work out that way. First, last, and always he was concerned with dancing ability. If a girl was able to convince him that she had a basic background in ballet, was an excellent tap dancer, met the height requirements, and was willing and able to submerge her own personality for the good of the team—then she was hired. Beauty was an added dividend.

During his years at the Music Hall, Markert always referred to the Rockettes as "my dancing daughters." In 1978 he was willing to defer a bit to his seventy-nine years by altering the sobriquet to "my dancing daughters . . . and granddaughters." According to the Rockettes themselves, past and present, he was very much like a second father to them. Evelyn Ashley, who joined the Rockettes in 1942 as the first permanent replacement to the original 1932 line, sums up the special relationship between Russell and the Rockettes this way:

> First of all, he was a perfectionist. But he was also very much like a father figure to us. We loved him. Yet, we were all a little bit scared of him. I mean, he could be very, very stern when he wanted to be. In those days, none of us dared to be seen around the theater or even going out the stage door if we were wearing slacks. Russell just didn't approve. He considered slacks very unladylike.
>
> But, like a father, if he thought a girl had personal problems he'd invite her to talk about them in the privacy of his office. He was always doing things like helping the girls to find better places to live or fixing them up with roommates so they wouldn't be lonely if they had just got into town. I'm sure the Rockettes today miss his guidance. I don't think the bunch now are as close as we all were in our day.

Markert explains that the "family" idea has always been important to him in both a personal and professional sense. In auditioning a girl for the Rockettes, he was always interested in her family background. He viewed it important to know if she grew up in a family who pampered and spoiled her or if she was required to help with the housework and pull a bit of her own weight inside the home environment. To him, a girl who was not used to contributing to the work around her home would, over the long haul, find it difficult to immerse herself in the total teamwork concept of the Rockettes. There can be no individual stars in the Rockettes.

From the beginning, Russell's concept of the dance line was precision—*absolute precision!* The idea was for the audience to see thirty-six girls, in intricate routines, moving as one dancer. Everything—the height, costumes, steps, even the skin tone—must be uniform. To achieve this end, the girls he hired would have to be able to dance magnificently and discipline themselves like nuns. It was hardly an easy challenge.

Three of the most famous Rockettes in Music Hall history are Vera Ellen, who was a Hollywood dancing star of major magnitude in the fifties; Lucille Bremer, who became a successful film star following her appearance as Judy Garland's sister in the classic film *Meet Me in St. Louis;* and Maria Beale Fletcher, who went on to become Miss America. Another Rockette, Sherry Patecell Lovejoy, won the Miss New York State Beauty Pageant. Markert found them all excellent dancers whose outside ambitions didn't interfere with their work as Rockettes. All of them were acceptable, that is, except one.

"You know," he smiles, "Vera Ellen was an excellent dancer and a nice looking girl. But if I wanted the arms to go up like this [he demonstrates, medium high] she'd put hers up like this [he demonstrates, raising them to eye level], so that she would stand out. She always wanted to exaggerate everything to her own way.

"One day I said to her, 'Look, Vera, we can't go on like this. If you do things like I want you to, it's fine.' So she said, 'What am I doing wrong?' So I said, 'Well, you're exaggerating everything.' She said, 'What do you mean by that?' I explained to her that I thought she was showing off, wanting to stand out. I told her I'd give her a few more weeks, and if she couldn't get that calmed down within herself, then she'd have to give me her notice. So, she gave me her notice in a few weeks and went on to become a movie star."

By and large, Russell had excellent working relationships with his "dancing daughters" down through the years. In several instances he carried the father relationship to the point of "giving them away" in marriage. He was instrumental in naming his longtime Rockette and assistant director, Emily Sherman, to replace him when he left. He was also in strong support of the move to make Violet Holmes, a Rockette since 1946, the current director of the troupe.

He says today that he has no particularly favorite shows among the hundreds he produced at the Music Hall, although two special events stand out in his mind. Other than their traditional high kicks at the end of every turn, the single most famous Rockette routine involves their "Parade of the Wooden Soldiers." The "Wooden Soldiers" music came originally from a Russian revue of many years ago. In the routine, which is usually featured in the Christmas show, the Rockettes strut their stuff in precision stiffness dressed in storybook military uniforms. At the end, the entire line faces a cannon that fires on them with a realistic puff of smoke. The "blast from the cannon" proceeds to bowl them over, and the Rockettes fall stiffly backward to the stage in tempo and precision, like so many dominoes. Although terribly tricky, and even a bit dangerous for the dancers, the "Wooden Soldier" routine has become another Music Hall tradition.

"Of course," he smiles, "the most popular thing we've ever done are the eye-high kicks which are our trademark. A long time ago, I decided we should do something new, so I worked out a different routine for the end of the act. It was good, but you should have seen the letters I got! They all wanted to know why I took out the high kicks on the end. Well, that's the last time I ever did that. The kicks are just too popular. They're our trademark."

Markert's eyes also shine when he talks about what could be the greatest achievement of his Rockettes or, for that matter, just about any other American dance group. The year was 1937 and the Music Hall, like the nation at large, was dusting itself off from the dire financial effects of the Great Depression. The theater was rapidly gaining an international reputation as the World's Greatest Theater and the Rockettes had become the resident stars. The government of France, trying desperately to ignore the war clouds gathering on its eastern border, decided to stage the Paris Exposition . . . a *Gala de Dance*. It would feature a competition of great dance groups from all over the world. The Rockettes were invited by the French government to represent the United States.

With France paying the costs, they would sail over on the *Ile de France* and return on the *Normandy*. Markert was producing the current stage show at the Music Hall when the departure date

(RIGHT) **Russell demonstrates his old panache with a few impromptu steps at the Rockette Alumnae Ball in the summer of 1978. (Courtesy of Vito Torelli.)**

neared. He decided he couldn't leave any of his "dancing daughters" at home, and took the entire line of thirty-six girls plus the ten permanent replacements. He would have his greatest dance line ever . . . forty-six girls! The competition was being held at a large auditorium in Paris called the Grand Palais. Markert had been advised that French Army engineers were already in the process of enlarging the stage.

When they arrived at the Grand Palais and started to rehearse, Markert discovered the stage was still not wide enough to accommodate his line of forty-six Rockettes. He told the engineers they'd have to widen the stage even more and they obliged him. In the meantime, he was forced to rehearse the line at the Chalet Theatre—in an upstage-downstage configuration because that stage also wasn't wide enough to hold them all.

Markert was asked to give the judges and the packed audiences four separate shows, about a half hour apart. The first number was a graceful kicking routine in which the Rockettes wore chiffon pajamas. Next came a fast, rhythm tap dance with all forty-six girls working together like parts of a fine wristwatch. This was followed by another change of pace to the seductive music of "Begin the Beguine." Each time, the audience cheered and whistled in a tremendous ovation. But the best was yet to come.

He wanted to make the final number really spectacular and decided to do a march routine to the accompaniment of both John Philip Sousa numbers and some traditional French marching songs. The Rockettes were costumed in shocking-pink military uniforms that showed off their lovely long legs. On their heads they had military caps, replete with tall feathers. He brought them on in an ever-widening wedge formation down a flight of tall stairs at the back of the stage. There was tremendous applause throughout the various patterns of the march number.

"At the end of the routine," Markert recalls, "we gave them the French salute. All of a sudden the people in the audience started running down the aisles and climbing over the orchestra pit to try and get to the girls. We had a heck of a time getting things back in order. Finally, all the ushers and people in control of things got the audience calmed down again.

"Then, with the audience still cheering like crazy, we took our exit in just the opposite way we had come on . . . up the big staircase until there was only one girl left at the top. She turned and gave them the salute again and the people just screamed and yelled for a long time. We ended up winning the Grand Prix. It was quite an experience."

For years an argument has been raging among dance critics as to whether what the Rockettes do is art. Too often, people have tended to dismiss the Rockettes as just another chorus line. It would be well to remember that open competition at the Paris Exposition of 1937. Among the distinguished dance companies they "defeated" were the Ballets de Monte Carlo, a successor to Diaghilev's Ballet Russe, as well as the corps de ballet of the Paris Opera.

Winning the Grand Prix at the Paris Exposition, which was rather like an Olympics of the Dance, with each nation's flag being introduced before its representatives took the stage, was a tremendous promotional boost for the Radio City Music Hall. It was one of the really important events that helped launch the Music Hall as the number-one New York attraction for tourists, both foreign and domestic. The two weeks in Paris was also the first time in the history of the theater that the Rockettes were not on the bill at the Music Hall. Markert hired a dance team and a singing-instrumental act to fill in the Rockette time slot in their absence.

Markert retired to a peaceful site in Connecticut in June of 1971. The Rockettes surprised him with a special going-away party and a present that he calls "the best kept secret in the history of the Music Hall." Several days before he was scheduled to leave, he was preparing himself to go up to the rehearsal hall for a run-through of the routines for his final show. He reached for his tap shoes, which he expected to be in their usual place, and was shocked to find them missing. He searched the backstage area thoroughly and with growing anger. He was disgusted to think someone would stoop low enough to steal his old tap shoes when he was just about to retire.

Nobody seemed to know anything at all about the missing shoes, and he admits his thoughts were on the ugly side. The mystery was cleared up, to his amazement, at the Rockettes' farewell party in his honor. The girls had filched the shoes, taken them out and had them bronzed, and attached to a lovely plaque that they presented him. His eyes still get misty when he talks about it.

Asked why he chose to retire when he remains in such obviously good condition, he says he was tired at the time and thought he had done enough during his nearly fifty years in the business. He had developed an ulcer and felt he needed the rest to regain his good health. He also found it difficult to work within the rapidly declining budgets he was given. Dwindling audiences at the Music Hall and the rising costs of everything he needed in order to produce his kind of show had exhausted his patience. He still has nothing but the highest praise for Alton Marshall, president of Rockefeller Center, Inc., and Charles Hacker, executive vice president of the Music Hall. But he admits the pressure of lower budgets may have aggravated his ulcer and forced his resignation.

"I guess it may have had something to do with it," he nods. "I'm nearly seventy-nine now, I work out three times a week, my ulcer is fine and I can even have my martinis before dinner."

He's obviously still sentimental about his "dancing daughters" and the Music Hall, and tries to get into the city to catch the opening of every new show. The Rockettes know he's in the audience because he shows his encouragement with a special whistle they all recognize. What they miss is his old battle cry from the wings during the show, "Shake it up for Daddy, girls!" That's the inscription they put on his plaque with the bronzed tap shoes, along with the signature "Your Dancing Daughters."

In 1977, the city of New York and Mayor Abraham Beame honored Russell Markert by presenting him with a special certificate of appreciation that read: "To Russell Markert, who gave New York City and the World one of the most popular entertainments in history . . . the Fabulous Rockettes. He founded and trained this precision dance group which opened Radio City Music Hall in 1932. They have since danced for more than 250 million people."

SEVEN

"DUFFEY"

No history of the Radio City Music Hall would be complete without the story of Muriel Kilduff. She held no grandiose position, but her contributions to the great theater in Manhattan lasted longer than just about anybody except Leonidoff and Markert. Now married, Muriel Kilduff has happily become Muriel Hake. But to her friends at the Music Hall she will always be "Duffey," the nickname given her by Russell Markert.

Duffey Hake has a recurring dream these days. She's in the Rockettes' dressing room and can't find her costume. The assistant stage manager has already given the "On Stage" call, and she isn't ready to go on. She also gets occasional twitches in her shapely legs around ten-thirty every morning. The sensations don't alarm her.

Although she is now retired, Duffey Hake remains the *compleat* Rockette. She's an attractive, mature woman with an almost unlined face beneath her softly coiffed blonde hair. In street clothes her body is as trim and slim as most women half her age. It's difficult to believe that she decided to become an ex-Rockette in January of 1971 when she was four months past her sixtieth birthday!

"Oh, I hadn't danced outside of the rehearsal hall for a few years when I retired," she reminds you. "I was busy enough as the captain of the Rockettes. The last time I stepped in and actually danced in a show was right before the strike in September of 1967. I guess I would have been fifty-seven years old then."

To anyone who has seen the Rockettes' strenuous routines, the eye-high kicks and the fast-paced tap dancing, the idea of a fifty-seven-year-old woman participating in them seems beyond belief. But Duffey is a remarkable woman and, without question, every modern-day Rockette's personal and professional model of perfection. Only the man who started it all, Russell Markert, can claim more time with the famed troupe.

Duffey wasn't one of the original Missouri Rockets in St. Louis, but she did join them a short time later when they toured Chicago. That was at the time when Markert wanted to form another troupe of Rockets so they could play two Balaban and Katz theaters in the Windy City at the same time. She so impressed Markert that he invited her to become one of his permanent group of American Rockets and she traveled on with them to New York. She was all ready to join them in the Joe Cook show on Broadway when the group was discovered by Roxy and brought into his new Roxy Theatre. She stayed at the Roxy, taking time out to join Russell on his film ventures in Hollywood, until it was time to become an original Rockette at the Radio City Music Hall in late 1932.

They were given a two-week rehearsal period for the opening show at the Music Hall, and Duffey clearly remembers her first impression of the great new theater and the opening night. "When we first saw the Music Hall," she recalls, "I think we were all struck by how different it was. Actually, I suppose most of us thought the Roxy Theatre was prettier. We loved the lobby and lounges, but none of us cared much for the auditorium when we first set eyes on it. It probably seems pretty silly now, but we thought the auditorium with that big curved ceiling looked like a tremendous airplane hangar. Of course, we first saw it with only the work lights. We changed our minds when we saw it in its full glory."

The Rockettes, still going under the title Roxyettes, were strictly an "act" when they went into the Music Hall. In other words, the girls had no contract with the Music Hall or even Roxy, for that matter. They worked exclusively for Russell Markert. Today Duffey laughs when she is asked if she ever dreamed in 1932 that her "run" at the Music Hall would last thirty-eight years. She reminds you that dancers, even in those early years, seldom looked far into the future. They simply enjoyed what they were doing and hoped it would continue.

She admits to having more than a little concern after the opening night. She remembers the first

(LEFT)
One of the most often repeated Music Hall shows is the "Undersea Ballet." Frank Spencer rendered this costume sketch for the August 1956 production with the instructions that the mermaid's hair should be "fluorescent pistacchio." (Courtesy of Frank Spencer.)

(BELOW)
A truly spectacular design is this 1958 octopus costume created by Frank Spencer for that year's production of the "Undersea Ballet," which played with the film *Auntie Mame*. (Courtesy of Frank Spencer.)

Frank Spencer created these robin costumes for the Rockettes in the Easter show of 1958. The "Chemise look" was high fashion that year, and Spencer managed to get a touch of the fashion in for his "birds." (Courtesy of Frank Spencer.)

The Rockettes have been transformed into any number of nonhuman objects over the years. They were zebras in the winter of 1956 as these Frank Spencer costume sketches illustrate. (Courtesy of Frank Spencer.)

Leon Leonidoff's summer production for the Music Hall in 1970 enabled Spencer to utilize his knowledge of the circus in this sketch of his clown costume for Alan Cole. (Courtesy of Frank Spencer.)

The late Albert Johnson rendered this beautiful sketch for a Fort McHenry set to be used as a background for "The Star Spangled Banner," a Leonidoff production of the 1940s. Unfortunately, the design was never executed. (Courtesy of James Morcom.)

Vincente Minnelli painted this striking sketch for a Spanish Flamenco production during his tenure as Music Hall art director in 1933. (Courtesy of Vincente Minnelli.)

(LEFT)
**Marco Montedoro came over from the *Folies Bergere* and the *Casino de Paris* to join
Roxy Rothafel at his Roxy Theatre and the Music Hall as costume designer.
This undated "champagne glass" costume was created in the early years.
(Courtesy of James Morcom.)**

(RIGHT)
**As a young Paris artist, Marco Montedoro had once hired the legendary spy Mata Hari as
his model. Perhaps he had her in mind when he created this seductively feminine
gown for a Music Hall production during the 1930s or 1940s. (Courtesy of James Morcom.)**

(LEFT)
This Latin dancing costume sketched by Marco Montedoro could possibly have been used in an early production of Ravel's "Bolero." (Courtesy of James Morcom.)

(RIGHT)
A sketch of a pert Montedoro Rockette costume created for the Music Hall between 1932 and 1946. (Courtesy of James Morcom.)

Morcom served in a dual capacity again in 1949, designing both sets and costumes for
the Markert production of "Top Hat and Tails." Note the cleverly misspelled advertising signs
in this sketch of Times Square. (Courtesy of James Morcom.)

(ABOVE)
James Morcom designed the setting and the costumes for Russell Markert's production "Pass the Peacepipe" in 1948. This is his original sketch for the setting. (Courtesy of James Morcom.)

(RIGHT)
Morcom's Indian costume sketch for "Pass the Peacepipe" in 1948. (Courtesy of James Morcom.)

(FAR RIGHT)
Specifically top hat and tails are the Rockette costumes in this Morcom sketch for the production of the same name in 1949. (Courtesy of James Morcom.)

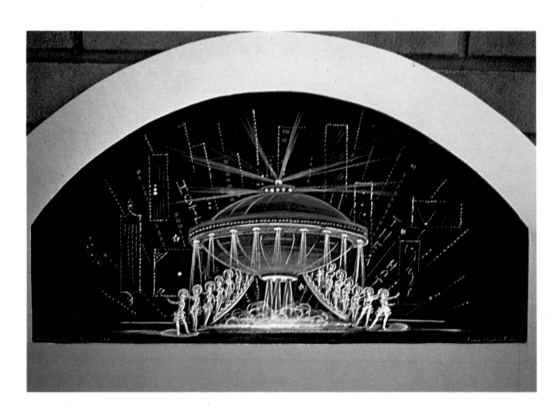

(ABOVE)
Creating a windmill and a field of tulips was Morcom's design problem in this 1960 sketch of a Leonidoff production called "Tulip Time." A photograph of the actual production appears elsewhere in these pages. (Courtesy of James Morcom.)

(OPPOSITE PAGE TOP)
The Rockettes descend from a flying saucer in this Jimmy Morcom scenery sketch for the 1967 production called "UFO." (Courtesy of James Morcom.)

(OPPOSITE PAGE BOTTOM)
Morcom re-created the feeling of the Louisiana bayous in this 1971 sketch for the Markert production number "Chloe." The actual setting was eventually painted by John Keck who followed Morcom as Music Hall art director. (Courtesy of James Morcom.)

CHRISTMAS '76   THE FINALE

(ABOVE)
A brilliant Christmas tree dominates the stage in this John Keck painting for the set
of "Snowflakes," a Peter Gennaro production in 1976. (Courtesy of John Keck.)

(OPPOSITE PAGE TOP)
John Keck's lovely scenery sketch for Leon Leonidoff's last production at the
Music Hall, *Saluda a Colombia*, in 1974. (Courtesy of John Keck.)

(OPPOSITE PAGE BOTTOM)
This John Keck design painting shows the setting for John Jackson's production called
La Fantasie du Cirque which was staged at the Music Hall in 1976. (Courtesy of John Keck.)

(ABOVE)
The Rockettes are anything but scantily clad as
they rehearse outdoors in very cold weather
in front of Macy's department store in preparation
for their appearance in the Thanksgiving Day
Parade. (Courtesy of Vito Torelli.)

(LEFT & BELOW)
Two shots of the famed Rockette "Wooden Soldier"
routine, from productions in 1957 and 1960.
(Courtesy of James Morcom.)

These stop-action photographs by Vito Torelli dramatically illustrate the physical difficulty of the Rockettes's most famous routine. A puff of smoke belches forth from the Santa Claus cannon as the Wooden Soldiers line up in single file in front of it. The invisible "cannonball" sends the first soldier tumbling into the one behind, and the entire line of dancers proceeds to fall, one after another, like so many dominoes. (Courtesy of Vito Torelli.)

(BELOW)
Live Rockettes dance beneath a huge photograph of themselves on the Music Hall stage in 1961. The Eastman color photomural, the largest ever made, had hung in New York's Grand Central Station. (Courtesy of James Morcom.)

(BOTTOM)
A Golden Sunburst is the theme of this Rockette routine staged in 1959. (Courtesy of James Morcom.)

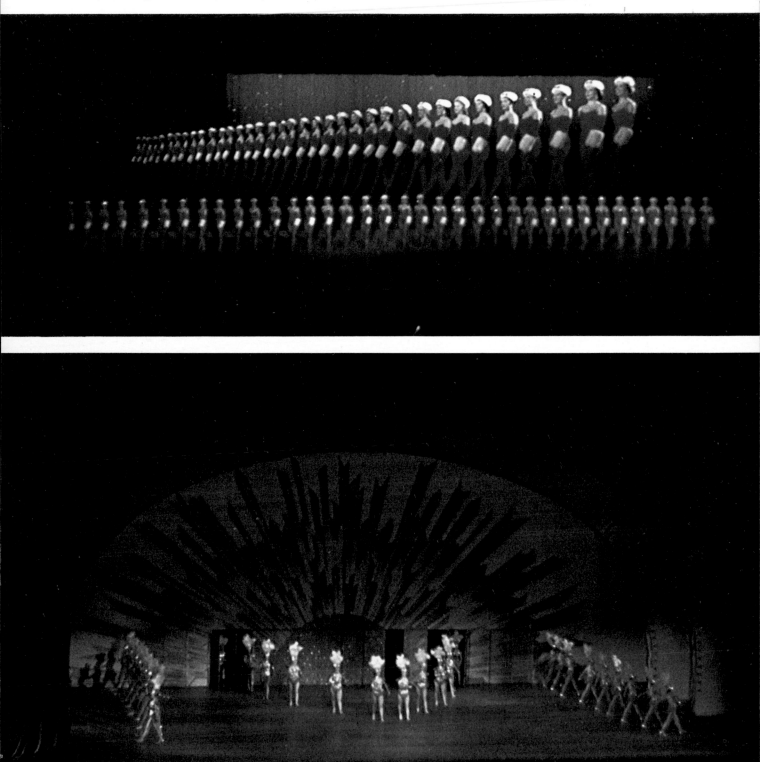

show as "disappointing." Duffey thinks the major problem was the overabundance of big-name stars on the first bill. With all the encores they received the program seemed to drag on endlessly. She remembers seeing the number of empty seats increase as the evening wore on. There was a heavy pall of gloom backstage after the opening night. According to Duffey, there were no opening night parties. She, at least, simply went home and climbed into bed.

There have been many changes at the Music Hall since 1932, and Duffey Hake has seen them all. Working conditions for the Rockettes have changed the most. The starting salary of the original Rockettes was fifty-five dollars a week. In the 1930s, with a new show being produced every week, Duffey remembers spending almost all but her sleeping hours in the Music Hall. In those days, the Rockettes would be rehearsing the new show in the hours between their four performances a day (sometimes five) of the current show. In productions where special scenery was featured, such as grand staircases too large to use in the rehearsal hall, the girls were required to stay after the final showing of the movie to rehearse on stage. That meant there was little time for a good night's sleep before reporting early the next morning for another grueling day of rehearsals and performances.

In 1947 Duffey was promoted to assistant captain, and a few years later was given the title "captain of the line." That job entailed being a special assistant to Russell and Emily Sherman. The job suited her. Markert had always admired her talent and teaching ability, taking her with him on his Hollywood expedition to train the West Coast dancers in his technique. As captain, she was required to fill a spot in the line when a girl became ill or was otherwise unavailable because of some emergency.

(LEFT) **Muriel Kilduff "Duffey" Hake in the summer of 1978. She danced as a Rocket, a Roxyette, and a Rockette for a total of forty-three years. (Courtesy of Vito Torelli.)**

(RIGHT) **To the right in this picture, perched atop the rehearsal piano, Captain "Duffey" Hake joins accompanist Beulah Cranston, Assistant Director Emily Sherman, and Russell Markert in a planning session in the early 1950s. (Courtesy of Henry Rapisarda-Cosmo-Sileo, Inc.)**

This posed difficulties for her. Russell had waived his stringent height requirements when he hired her in Chicago. She was only five feet three and a half inches tall . . . an inch and a half shorter than his standards then. But he had admired her talent and attitude too much to turn her down. As captain, among the taller girls of the 1950s and 1960s, she was hard-pressed to step into routines designed for the shortest girls while simultaneously teaching still another routine to the taller girl she had replaced.

On one occasion, feeling a trifle insecure before going onstage as a last-minute replacement, she decided to check with the girl who was next to her in line. She asked the girl on the left the name of the girl on her right, and was astounded when the Rockette said she hadn't really noticed. The Rockettes, fiercely concentrating on perfecting their own precise timing, were often oblivious of those working next to them in the long line. From that point on, Duffey made it a practice to keep exact charts of the lineups in each formation. The practice continues today.

Duffey has also been in an ideal position to obtain firsthand knowledge of the growth of American womanhood over the past forty years or so . . . at least growth from the personally physical point of view. In the beginning, she says, the Rockettes ranged from five five to five seven and a half in height. Creating the illusion of uniformity in height has always been carried out in the same way . . . the tallest Rockettes dance in the center of the line with the shorter girls going down, stair-step fashion, to the ends of the line. Today, the Rockettes measure from five five and a half to five nine.

As captain, it was part of Duffey's job to see that the costumes were all in order and ready for the next day's performances. She has been especially amazed at the way the shoe sizes have increased over the years.

"In the old days," she laughs, "most of the girls wore shoes that were maybe threes or fours or fives or five and a halfs. When I left, the girls were wearing anything from sevens to ten and a halfs. It's just amazing the way young women are getting bigger as time goes by."

Muriel "Duffey" Kilduff Hake is extremely proud of her years as a Rockette. In the very earliest days of the American Rockets the dancers encouraged Markert to new heights in his aim for perfection

Retired Rockettes flash their old form in a special routine for the Rockette Alumnae Ball. They laughingly bill themselves as "The Breathless Twelve." (Courtesy of Vito Torelli.)

New York's Lieutenant Governor Mary Anne Krupsak was the guest of honor at the Rockette Alumnae Association's twenty-third charity ball in July of 1978. "Duffey" Hake (left) presents Krupsak with a special award in recognition of her efforts to save the Music Hall from demolition. (Courtesy of Vito Torelli.)

in unison dancing. Markert would apparently say, "Make a mistake in this routine and you can just keep on dancing . . . right out the stage door." Duffey says the Rockets not only made few unnecessary mistakes, but also kept asking Russell to give them bigger challenges, more difficult routines.

It doesn't seem surprising to her that she was still able to dance on the Music Hall stage at the age of fifty-seven. She admits that the physical stress became more extreme as her age increased, but the excitement made up for the pain. Her biggest difficulty in actively stepping into the line was the anxiety she felt about the lack of proper rehearsal time.

In a sense, the Music Hall was also the foundation of her marriage. In 1955 she met her future husband, Bob Hake, through a reporter who was dating a fellow Rockette. Hake is an editor with the Associated Press, and the AP building is conveniently situated at the eastern end of the Radio City Music Hall. The romance flourished and the writer and the dancer were married about a year after their first meeting.

Although she retired in 1971, Duffey is still active with the Rockettes. In 1955, Rockette "Dinkey" Mayer came up with an exciting idea. Recognizing that the Rockettes had been a sorority as much as a dance team through the years, she decided to organize a Rockette Alumnae Association. Miss

Mayer took the idea to Markert who gave his OK but warned that he was much too busy with his work to get actively involved in it. The association became an immediate hit and now has more than three hundred members who live in nearly every state in the union and several foreign countries. Duffey Hake is vice-president of the association, and is scheduled to move up to the president's chair.

The Rockette Alumnae Association has kept news of the Music Hall very much in the daily lives of its members. Its first big charity ball was held in the Waldorf Astoria's Empire Room in the spring of 1956, and the former Rockettes have been steady contributors to worthwhile charity since that time. The original charity ball was held to raise funds for the aid of retarded children. (Many former Rockettes, by the way, teach in schools for retarded children, since exceptional children, by and large, respond eagerly to dancing and movement.)

While the proceeds of the annual Spring Ball go to the Retarded Children's Fund, an annual November luncheon raises money for other worthy causes. Part of the proceeds of the luncheon go for the care of a former Rockette who suffered an accident that left her paralyzed from the waist down. Another portion goes each year for a Julliard Scholarship in Russell Markert's name, and the rest is divided up among a number of nationally known charities.

Several of the original Missouri Rockets are alive and well in St. Louis. They and other members of the first Rockette troupe at the Music Hall love to join their sisters at the alumnae gatherings. Always in the center of things is the woman who saw them all, with few exceptions, come and go. Only Emily Sherman spent more time at the Music Hall. Otherwise, Muriel "Duffey" Kilduff Hake—from 1927 until 1961—outlasted them all.

EIGHT

LADIES AND GENTLEMEN ...THE ROCKETTES!

Perhaps you are one of the 250,000,000 people who have visited the Radio City Music Hall since it first opened in 1932. If so, chances are you have a vivid memory of your first experience there. Maybe it was long ago when you were small. You climbed down the steps of the crosstown bus at Sixth Avenue and Forty-ninth Street and clung to your mother's hand as she guided you toward Fiftieth. It was cold and you had to wait in a long line, but your mother assured you it would be warm inside and you'd love the big Christmas show.

Or possibly your first view of the great showplace came after a tiring cross-country trip and a hot, humid day of gawking at the view from the lofty heights of the Empire State Building. You'd driven through Chinatown and Greenwich Village and had even made the tortuous climb to the crown of the Statue of Liberty. Still, you weren't prepared for the wonder of the Music Hall. It seems logical that the Radio City Music Hall is one of the few childhood memories that hasn't shrunk with the passage of time.

Once inside the building, you undoubtedly experienced the awe everyone save the most jaded feels in the face of such elegance and size. The huge auditorium took your breath away with its spaciousness. You thrilled to the sound of the great Wurlitzer organ and watched with fascination as the contour curtain opened and gave you a look at live performers doing their work right before your eyes.

But the real "Magic Time" happens for most people when an offstage voice booms through the loudspeaker system . . . "Ladies and Gentlemen, the world-famous Radio City Music Hall Rockettes!" The eye is dazzled by the scene on the huge stage. Thirty-six gorgeous girls, beautifully costumed to show off seventy-two shapely legs, move through intricate dance patterns as though they were one. They move so well together, it is virtually impossible to pick out any one face. Still, you know they must all be truly beautiful. The excitement builds during their routine and the applause never fails to come when the Rockettes go into their show-stopping unison eye-high kicks.

In time you may forget the name of the movie playing on your first visit to the Music Hall. You may have difficulty remembering the other live acts on the bill as well as all the artistic glories of that magnificent building. But very few ever lose the memory of the Rockettes. They have become the living embodiment of the Radio City Music Hall. They exemplify the color and excitement that have become a Music Hall trademark for visitors from all over the world.

By the spring of 1978, when it looked like the great theater might close forever, some members of the media were dismissing the Music Hall and the Rockettes as an anachronism—a surviving throwback to a long-dead era in American history. Yet any sports fan has only to turn on his television set to see hundreds of Rockette-like girl cheerleader groups doing routines remarkably similar to the basic Music Hall style. Precision dancing by a long line of girls onstage may well be a dying art form, but the apparent need for it certainly is not.

Ask any Rockette, past or present, why she became a member of that line and the answer is nearly always the same. "It's what I wanted to do from the first time I visited the Music Hall." And no Rockette ever forgets her audition. Dee Dee Knapp, a young twelve-year veteran of the current troupe from Sylvan Beach in upstate New York, is an excellent example.

"Actually," she says, "I started dancing when I was three years old. Later, my dancing teacher began to take a bunch of us kids to study in New York. We'd always go to see the Rockettes while we were there. I came every summer for two weeks since I was about six. We'd stay in a hotel, take our lessons, and then go to the Music Hall as often as we could. I knew way back then that I wanted to be a Rockette.

"Finally, when I was sixteen and thought I was old enough and good enough, I sent in a picture and a history of my background and asked for an audition. When they finally agreed to give me one, I was so excited I could hardly stand it. My head was in such a whirl on the day of the audition that I almost got lost on the way from the hotel to the theater.

"By the time I got up to the rehearsal hall, I had calmed down enough to at least act like I was a professional. When they called my name, I got up and walked over to the piano player like a real star and handed him all my sheet music. Then I walked back to the center of the room and said, 'I want it played in three-quarter time,' actually snapping my fingers to give him the beat. I'm sure everybody sitting there must have thought I was insane, or something.

"Well, everything went fine until I had to do some kicks at the end. You see, I was so poor at the time I couldn't afford new tap shoes. The straps had broken and I thought I could hold my shoes on by putting these big rubber bands around them. Anyway, I started doing the kicks and I was putting everything I had into them . . . getting up really high. All of a sudden one of the rubber bands broke and my shoe went sailing way up into the air like a rocket. It nearly hit the great big ceiling light. Well! I was so embarrassed I could have just died. I had been trying to look so professional, and then this happens! There were about sixty or seventy other girls sitting there waiting to do their auditions, and the whole place cracked up.

"Russell Markert was still the director then and Emily was his assistant. He turned to Emily and said, 'We have to hire this girl. She obviously needs the money.' So, it turned out all right after all, and I got my job. Of course, I didn't start right away because Russell wouldn't let me. I was still in high

Veteran Rockette Dee Dee Knapp. Her audition didn't go as she had planned, but it was successful despite some unforeseen events. (Courtesy of Vito Torelli.)

Rockette Cindy Peiffer still treasures this Russell Markert letter announcing the date of her audition. (Courtesy of Cindy Peiffer.)

RADIO CITY MUSIC HALL
Rockefeller Center   New York 10020   CIrcle 6-460C

March 25, 1971

Miss Cindy Peiffer
Box 132 - Route 5
Ocean House Road
Cape Elizabeth, Maine 24107

Dear Miss Peiffer:

This is to advise you that an audition for the Rockettes will be held on Monday, April 19, 1971 at 2 PM o'clock.

Unless you are positive that you have all the necessary requirements, do not waste your money and time to attend the audition. Please keep in mind that an audition does not necessarily guarantee a position.

Please report to the 44 West 51st Street Stage Entrance and bring your tap shoes and rehearsal clothes. It is also necessary that you advise us whether or not you will attend. Please reply by April 10, 1971.

Yours very truly,

Russell Markert
RUSSELL MARKERT
Director of Rockettes

RM:dh

Rockettes walk the picket line outside the Music Hall during their strike in 1967.
(Courtesy of Vito Torelli.)

I'M A ROCKETTE I GET $4.12 A SHOW + REHEARSE 40 HRS. FOR NOTHING!

school, and Russell said he wanted me to graduate first and then he'd write and let me know when I'd start. Sure enough, he wrote me a year later, asked me to start, and I've been here ever since.''

Not all of the three thousand or so girls who have been members of the Rockette line had Dee Dee's unfortunate experience with their tap shoes. But each one vividly recalls every aspect of the grueling audition that meant a do-or-die chance to fulfill her life's ambition. Each will tell you that being a member of the troupe was an experience they wouldn't trade for anything, with the exception of marriage and children.

Through the years, about a third of the group has been born and raised in the city; the others come from nearly every state in the Union. Occasionally an exceptional dancer from a foreign country will be hired. In the 1950s, two English girls were members of the troupe at the same time. Nine times out of ten, a Rockette who leaves exchanges her bespangled costume for the marriage vows, although some have continued on as Rockettes for a time after marriage.

Although the job has elements of glamour and a Rockette achieves instant celebrity as soon as she announces her occupation, the work involved is extremely physical and the workday is necessarily long with no opportunity for overtime pay. Conditions have improved since the Rockettes joined the American Guild of Variety Artists union a number of years ago. Wages have also increased dramatically as a result of a six-week strike in 1967. The young women won a 33 percent increase over their basic ninety-six-dollar weekly pay along with fringe benefits. But the work load continues to be a tough one.

When the Music Hall decided to adopt a policy of showing movies early in 1933, it meant that all the performers and backstage people were on an endless carrousel of activity. In the first year, a movie played for exactly one week. With each new movie came a brand-new stage production. In other words, while the Rockettes were performing in the current show, they were also rehearsing

(TOP, RIGHT) **The dancers apply their makeup in one of two Rockette dressing rooms before taking the stage for a performance in the early 1940s. (Herbert Gehr, Life Magazine © 1942, Time, Inc.)**

(BOTTOM, RIGHT) **The Rockettes are fitted in their costumes for a new production in the early 1940s. (Herbert Gehr, Life Magazine © 1942, Time, Inc.)**

another show that would open the following week. The aforementioned film *Little Women* proved at the end of 1933 that a movie could draw large crowds for more than a week. In later years, blockbuster films would run for several weeks, thereby giving the Rockettes and other performers a chance to breathe a little easier during most of the run of a current show. Still, when a new production was scheduled to go on, it meant extra-full days of performance and rehearsal at the same time.

A Rockette of the 1970s has a normal work schedule like this: She reports to the theater between 10:00 and 11:00 A.M. for "half-hour" call before the curtain rises on the stage show. During this half hour, she applies her own stage makeup, gets into her costume, and performs her stretching exercises in preparation for the performance. At the conclusion of the performance, she has something like two hours free time while the motion picture is shown. Still, she can't stray too far from the Music Hall lest she get tied up in traffic and not return in time for the next show. During the course of the day she'll give four performances and won't be free to pursue either sleep or the New York night life until 10:30 P.M., or later.

On rehearsal weeks, the work schedule is increased. In addition to doing the current show, a Rockette must learn new routines and practice them until the director feels they measure up to the high Rockette standards set years ago by Russell Markert. Rehearsals usually last a minimum of three days and involve many hours of both physical and mental labor. Rehearsals are usually held in the large, mirrored rehearsal hall, which nearly approximates the important dimensions of the stage. They can be scheduled early in the morning before the first performance, between performances, and on rare occasions, when special scenery not a part of the current production is needed, following the final show of the evening.

During rehearsal week, a Rockette's day may begin three hours earlier than normal and end well after her usual nightly departure time. Dress rehearsal time is especially strenuous. On dress rehearsal day a Rockette is forced to rise at 6:00 A.M. or earlier in order to be made up, dressed, and ready to go onstage at 7:30 A.M. If the dress rehearsal goes well, she has a chance to rest a bit during the first showing of the new motion-picture attraction. Otherwise, it's back to the rehearsal hall to iron out the remaining kinks in the new production. There is no margin for error when they are ready to be introduced. Each Rockette is an important link in a precision chain that the public has come to expect to be flawless.

Appropriately, the current director and choreographer of the Rockettes is Violet Holmes, who joined the troupe as a dancer in 1945. In 1973, Violet replaced former Rockette Emily Sherman, who had filled in for the retired Russell Markert. She had followed Duffey Hake as captain when the latter retired in 1971. The Rockette hierarchy is obviously a closed corporation with advancement coming from within the ranks.

From personal experience, Violet Holmes stresses the need for every Rockette to familiarize herself with not only her own section of the routine, but also with that of the other girls. She calls this her opposite-foot theory. Because of their position in the line, half of the Rockettes must key their movements off the right foot, while the other half starts with the left. In the event of an emergency when a girl has to trade places with another, she must be completely familiar with the other's part of the routine. In the normal course of replacing each other in position because of the vacation and days-off schedule, a Rockette must be completely prepared to step into another place in the line on short notice.

Many days before a new show is set to go into rehearsal, the choreographer plots it all out on paper. Then she goes alone to the rehearsal hall to see if her paper-planning works in practice. She dances the routines alone, without musical accompaniment. In fact, she never hears the music she has

A group of Rockettes report for work at the Fifty-first Street stage entrance on a Sunday morning in 1978. (Courtesy of Vito Torelli.)

Rockette Director Violet Holmes demonstrates a step in front of the bar in the large rehearsal hall in the upper reaches of the theater building. Some of her dancers are reflected in the mirror that runs the length of the large room. (Courtesy of Bob Coogan.)

selected until actual rehearsals begin to the accompaniment of the Rockette's rehearsal pianist. Unless they attend an orchestra rehearsal, no one hears the complete orchestral arrangement of the music until dress rehearsal.

In recent years, the Music Hall has closed for several weeks at a time as an economy measure. After a hiatus, Holmes recognizes that the Rockettes inevitably have a lot to talk about concerning their adventures since they last saw each other. Accordingly, Holmes's first rehearsal always begins with an announcement . . . "Okay, girls. You have five minutes to talk." The enthusiastic conversation is seldom finished at the end of five minutes when the director then formally requests quiet in the rehearsal hall. As she puts it, "If all else fails, I use my whistle to get some order." The famed Holmes whistle is exactly like the ones used by football coaches, and is an object of good-humored hatred among the current crop of Rockettes.

Next comes a verbal explanation of the general theme of the routine, plus a description of the costumes, etc. That out of the way, the actual rehearsals begin . . . working out of the third position, the Rockettes might swing into a diagonal formation, then execute a rhumba, a tango, and a soft-shoe routine in rapid order before moving into the "lineup" for the traditional eye-high kicks.

Each rehearsal, following a hiatus, lasts for three hours; then there is a break for lunch; followed by another two or three hours of work. This schedule is carried through Monday, Tuesday, and Wednesday (when there's no show already in production) with dress rehearsal always set for Thursday morning, opening day. The choreographer must be the most active person in the room, never sitting, constantly going from girl to girl demonstrating and perfecting the individual steps. It's no wonder that Russell Markert retains his remarkable physical trim after nearly forty years at the Music Hall.

A few years ago, in another management move to save money, Markert's original forty-six-girl Rockette troupe was cut down to thirty-nine. Whereas the onstage line formerly included thirty-six girls at a time, today's line numbers only thirty. In the past there were always ten permanent replacements, or "swing girls." Today there are nine. The "swing girls" are necessary because of the Rockettes'

The full line of thirty-six Rockettes dances in front of James Morcom's remarkably realistic re-creation of the RCA Building during a production of the early 1950s. (Courtesy of Cosmo-Sileo Associates.)

working schedule. It's a tricky arrangement. Each Rockette works four consecutive seven-day weeks, then gets a week off, and returns to work three more consecutive seven-day weeks before she gets another full week off. In this constant shuffling, each member of the line must be prepared to step in anywhere, consistent with her height.

As mentioned before, part of the Rockettes' mystique concerns their apparent sameness in height. Markert was always a stickler on the height question. Many would-be Rockettes tried to fool him at their auditions by wearing bouffant hairdos to make themselves appear taller. Markert solved the problem by ordering a measuring chart painted on the door of the rehearsal hall. If there was any question about a young woman's height, he'd order her to stand against the door and would probe her hairdo with a pencil to find the exact measurement. Although the tallest girls may tower three and a half inches over their shorter sisters, the illusion is sustained by placing the short girls at the end of the line with the taller ones in the center. Today, the illusion is furthered by matching the line by shoulder height as well. In the old days, the hemlines of the costumes matched perfectly despite the elevation of the girl wearing it.

When the Music Hall was built, Roxy insisted it should be a livable city unto itself. Incorporated into the backstage area is a twenty-six-bed dormitory for the young women who can't get home to sleep, a hospital staffed by a trained nurse, a cafeteria, tailor shop, and numerous other amenities to give the Music Hall a feeling of home. In recent years, much of the services have been shut down due to financial cutbacks in the overall operation. The Rockettes occupy huge dressing rooms on two floors. A third is available when needed. All dressing rooms are equipped with showers.

Civil libertarians have on occasion tried to make an issue of the fact that no black woman has ever been a Rockette. The issue never amounted to much when it was proved that black performers worked in other areas of the Music Hall show, and that neither race nor place of origin had anything to do with employment with the Rockettes. From the beginning, the flesh tones of his dancers were every bit as important to Markert as their dancing skills and measurements. If his "dancing machine" was to look and move like one girl, there could be no startling differences in their general appearance. No one could be permitted to "stand out" in any way.

To illustrate the point, veteran Rockette Susan Boron nearly lost her job a few years ago because she spent her week off on the beaches of sunny Florida. One of Markert's still-existing rules prohibits the acquisition of suntans of any shade. When Boron returned from her vacation, feeling healthy although not deeply tanned, Markert took one look at her, reminded her of the rules, and suspended her. She apologized and managed to cajole him into agreeing on a twenty-dollar bet that she could lose the tan in two weeks.

She returned to her native Niles, Ohio, intent on winning the bet as well as getting her job back. She not only stayed out of the sun, but also decided to help nature along in her fading process. She took milk baths, buttermilk baths, and every other remedy guaranteed to fade a suntan. Progress was painfully slow. Finally, she decided to use drastic methods and liberally applied a special bleaching cream to all her tanned areas. The next morning the result of the bleaching cream was astonishing. She hadn't got lighter—only larger. The cream had an adverse reaction on her skin, causing it to swell. Still, her swelling and the tan disappeared within the two-week period and she was reinstated in her job.

This passion for uniformity is the public hallmark of the Rockettes, prompting some critics to refer to them as "dancing automatons." However, Russell Markert always countered this criticism by explaining that precision dancing required a submersion of individuality. In his view, the "girls still have their faces and their individual personalities." Of course, it's not easy to spot those individual faces from

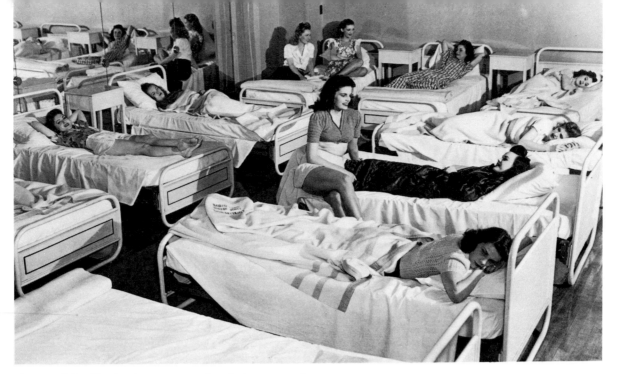

Some of the Rockettes nap or relax between performances in their special Music Hall dormitory in this 1947 photo. (Courtesy of Cosmo-Sileo Associates.)

a seat in the huge auditorium. That possibly explains why the Rockettes have not been particularly pursued by "stage-door Johnnies" down through the years. In fact, their two most loyal fans are elderly gentlemen who have caught nearly every opening for a number of years. They have showered the young women with record albums and other goodies from time to time, but no "stage-door romance" seems imminent.

But the Rockettes don't feel they are simply lost in a crowd. Each girl performs her routines in association with her peers, but in her mind, she is the center of attention. As Violet Holmes says, "Our girls don't have to feel like they're competing with somebody else on stage. We have no stars. Better still, all our girls are stars!"

The feeling of teamwork and comradeship continues past the time they actually spend on stage. The togetherness of the thirty-nine modern-day Rockettes seems as close as that of the forty-six girls of 1932, despite any natural skepticism a college housemother might feel after comparing her own coterie of young charges. In the old $55-per-week days, many of the Rockettes stayed at the Rehearsal Club, a home away from home for aspiring young actresses and dancers. Today, a Rockette with seniority can earn a salary of $304 per week. She can also make as much as $45 extra per week when she performs with the augmented ballet company. Under the improved financial conditions, many of the dancers choose another Rockette as a roommate and rent East Side Manhattan apartments.

The Rockettes who worked in the line with Maria Beale Fletcher when she was crowned Miss America were as proud of her as if they had won the honor themselves. When Miss Fletcher came to New York on her tour, she was welcomed backstage with girlish delight. The Rockettes still considered her one of them. Similarly, when a former director at the Music Hall became overly waspish about the brilliant color of one girl's rehearsal togs, it was decided that an immediate show of unity was the best response. All thirty-six Rockettes purchased the exact same costume and wore it to rehearsal the following day.

The Rockettes of the World War II years still chuckle over a story they claim is factual and indicative of their sisterly relationship. Nylon stockings were considered a luxurious and virtually unat-

In the "good old days" the Music Hall cast and crew could purchase good hot food in the theater's own cafeteria. Economy restrictions forced the closing of the cafeteria several years ago. (Courtesy of Cosmo-Sileo Associates.)

tainable commodity in those years of war shortages. They were also considered a most vital part of any properly dressed woman's attire. In time, the forty-six dancers had only one wearable pair among them. The tops of the stockings were tattered and torn, but the part that covered the famous calves was perfect. For a long time, each of the forty-six members of the troupe reportedly took turns wearing the same pair of stockings for important social occasions.

World War II took the Rockettes out of the Music Hall for the first time since the Paris Exposition. They continued to do their regular shows in the great theater, but would hop on trains and buses for excursions to the Army Air Corps base at Pawling, New York, or head crosstown for a big War Bond Rally at Madison Square Garden, or join Bob Hope and other stars for special appearances at the Stage Door Canteen.

The first really commercial appearance for the troupe outside of the Music Hall came during the early days of New York television when they were hired for an appearance on a Mary Martin special. The management warned them that the TV work would require a great deal of extra time in addition to their daily stage appearances, but the Rockettes voted to go ahead. Some of them began to doubt the wisdom of their decision after the first day. The combination of traveling back and forth between the Music Hall and the studio in Brooklyn for all-night sessions and doing four live performances a day as well as the TV show, meant that most of them went three days and nights without more than a few minutes of sleep at a time.

For years the Macy's Thanksgiving Day Parade has offered the general public an opportunity to see the Rockettes without paying the price of admission at the Music Hall. In recent years, of course, the event has been televised nationally. In the early years the girls rode on a float for the length of the parade and then performed one of their routines as a special feature in front of Macy's in Herald Square. On one particularly cold Thanksgiving Day the scantily clad dancers nearly suffered frostbite. They were promised that the situation would be remedied "next year."

The following year the girls were delighted to find they would be riding on a heated float enclosed in plastic. Unfortunately, as in "The Three Bears," this arrangement proved to be much too hot. It was a group of nearly asphyxiated Rockettes who staggered out from under their plastic bubble and tried to form their traditional straight line. In recent years the potholes in the street in front of the department store have made their precision chores even more difficult than usual.

It was during the mid-1970s that appearing outside the Music Hall became something of a regular thing for the Rockettes. Beset with financial problems, the Music Hall decided to abandon its policy of four shows a day, seven days a week, for fifty-two weeks in the year. It was simply a matter of economics. The management found it more expedient to close the theater for a few weeks at a time, or rent it out for rock concerts, jazz festivals, ice shows, etc., than to keep it open with the traditional program.

Again, acting collectively, the Rockettes approached the management with a startling idea. "Can we have permission to go out on our own and book shows outside of New York?" There was one big flaw in the plan. The Music Hall legally owns the name *Rockettes*. The girls would not be allowed to use the name on their own. They formed their own corporation under the name Precision Dancers Unlimited, Inc. The first (and last) date under the new title was in Springfield, Massachusetts. The show proved to be a hit, but the group was disbanded because of the logistics involved in transporting more than thirty young women from place to place on "bus and truck" tours.

The Music Hall management finally came up with a plan that would allow the Rockettes to work elsewhere when the great theater was closed for regular periods. The girls would still be required to perform under the Music Hall aegis. Under the new setup they were quickly seen on national television with two appearances on Howard Cosell's ABC variety show as well as in showplaces other than their

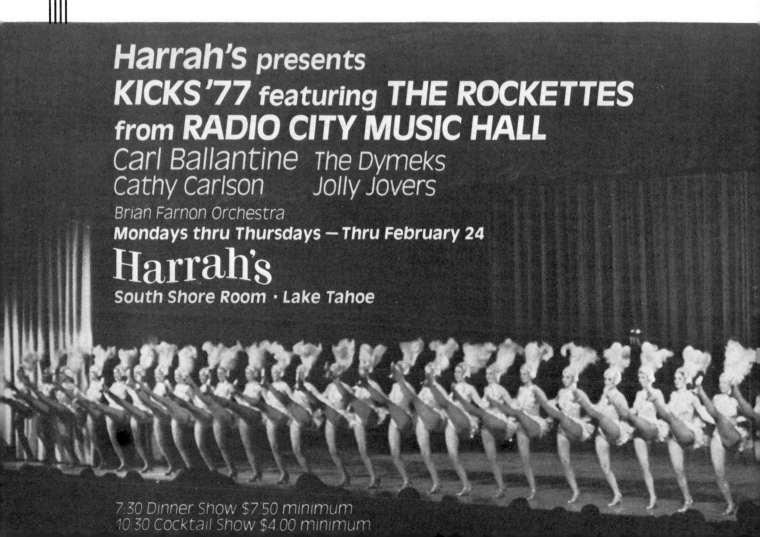

Thirty girls—Count 'em!—Thirty girls! The Rockettes line up for press photographers along Fisherman's Wharf in San Francisco. They had taken a sight-seeing trip from their duties as the special attraction at Lake Tahoe. (Courtesy of Diane Knapp.)

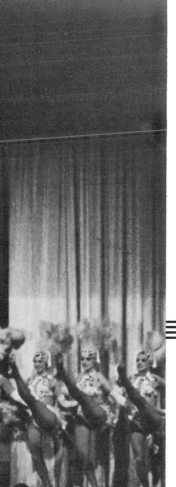

A special postcard honors the Rockettes during their 1977 appearance at Harrah's Club in Lake Tahoe, Nevada. (Courtesy of Harrah's, Reno, Nevada.)

home base. Nevada's plush gambling casinos and hotels became a temporary home during their hiatus time at the Music Hall. They played Harrah's South Shore Room at Lake Tahoe in 1976 as the star attraction of an entire show produced by the Music Hall. The following year Harrah's wanted them again—this time alone.

They also took Nevada's largest city by storm when they were booked into the Las Vegas Hilton. In a city where the chorus lines are usually topless and the routines not always spectacular, the wholesome Rockettes proved to be a popular eye-opener. They shared billing on the hotel's marquee with Glen Campbell and others for a period of four weeks. Their popularity in the desert caused the Music Hall to hire and train more girls to replace the regular line until they returned. There are standing offers for the Rockettes to appear in any number of places. Most of the offers must be refused because of their schedule at the Showplace of the Nation.

While the yellowed advertisements for the Music Hall opening prove that S. L. "Roxy" Rothafel was very much the star attraction back in 1932, the Rockettes have danced their way into that unofficial billing in the intervening years. The feature film always gets first billing in modern-day ads, but the Rockettes follow closely behind. They are the undoubted stars of *every* stage production at the Music Hall.

In May of 1978, the recognition became official in a John Jackson production at the Music Hall. For the first time, the Rockettes were assigned more than their usual one routine of three to five minutes in length. In that production they dominated the stage in not one, but *three* featured production numbers.

An anachronism? A throwback to a bygone era? Or an unusually wholesome and harmonious group of thirty-nine young women? Perhaps all the appellations fit in one degree or another. Over the years they have been costumed as astronauts, dolls, wooden soldiers, horses, bonbons out of a candy box, tables and chairs, poodles, cigars emerging from a giant cigar box, and every manner of flora and fauna and what-have-you. They remain a unique link in the chain of modern dance. Through hard work and dedication they have earned the title . . . the World-Famous Radio City Music Hall Rockettes!

NINE

THE MUSIC MEN —AND WOMEN

The five-minute call before the curtain could very well be "Man your boats." When the Radio City Music Hall Symphony Orchestra readies itself to go on, the procedure is not unlike a crew scrambling aboard a seagoing vessel. In a strange-shaped enclosure below stage level, with a rounded front wall and no ceiling, sits the celebrated mechanism known as the orchestra bandwagon. When the call is given, the formally clad orchestra members clamber up a number of portable wooden staircases that act as gangplank entrances to the wagon. On cue, the elevating platform starts upward and the audience gets its first view of one of the oldest continuing symphony orchestras in America.

Certainly the New York Philharmonic and orchestras of some other major cities were formed on an earlier date, but none of them can top the Music Hall Symphony in sheer number of performances: a minimum of four a day, seven days a week, fifty-two weeks a year for nearly fifty years. Since December 27, 1932, it has been the "Music" in the Music Hall. Although reduced in numbers, the orchestra joins the Rockette line as the only continuing performing body at the Music Hall since the grand opening.

From the beginning, the Music Hall music department has been a large and spectacular organization with its resident music director, associate conductors, staff composers and arrangers, staff organists, Glee Club, Choral Groups, and librarian. In the beginning it included some of the great names in American music, as well as others who grew to fame in later years.

Veteran members of the Music Hall family speak in tones of hushed reverence when they refer to the original musical director, Erno Rapee. They say he was a master musician who set the standards they have tried to follow through the years. Rapee had come over to the Music Hall with most of his staff from the Roxy Theatre. They were artists Roxy trusted and considered the best in the business. They shared his dream of making the Music Hall something more than just another theater. Rapee brought in musicians who could perform, on a single program, music ranging from Beethoven to Berlin. The orchestra would furnish the backing for opera excerpts, the ballet, the Rockettes, Glee Club, and guest artists in special spots, in addition to contributing its own selections before and during the show.

Earle Moss was one of the standout members of that group of excellent staff arrangers who began work many weeks before the official Music Hall opening in 1932. He spent a total of eighteen years at the big theater on Fiftieth Street. Today he lives in retirement in Maryville, Missouri. Although in his late seventies, Moss still has a twinkle in his eye and a verbal wit to match it, and excellent recall of the early years. Moss is still in awe of Rapee's musical ability and says the Hungarian-born composer, conductor, and orchestrator had "a natural talent which is not given to many of us."

"I suppose most people don't realize it," he says, "but Mr. Rapee wrote the songs 'Diane' and 'Charmaine' when he was musical director for Warner Brothers in the early days of the film business. I can remember having played his orchestration of 'Tamborin Chinoise' long before I had ever met him and thinking how marvelously clever it was. I later asked him about it and he said he had written it in just two days because he was hungry and needed the money.

"Rapee used to astound me sometimes. He had a photographic eye and a computer mind. One time, I came into his office at the Music Hall to submit a score for his examination. He was busy so I just placed the score on his desk, upside down, and waited for him to finish. Finally he looked up, saw the score, and said, 'Well, Moss, what have you got there?' I told him it was the score to 'so-and-so,' a pop tune he had probably never heard of. He took a glance at the first page, which was still upside down. Then he put a finger on a certain bar and said, 'In the second horn here didn't you mean E *flat* instead of E *natural?*' That is just a sample of his visual dexterity. He had spotted a mistake instantly— even with the score page *upside down!*"

Moss is also lavish in his praise of Roxy, crediting him to be such a good judge of talent that he was responsible for the successful careers of Rapee, Leonidoff, Patricia Bowman, Jan Peerce, and many others outside the Music Hall. Earle is quick to elucidate his belief that a "broken heart" was as much the cause of the great showman's death as a coronary. Roxy, Moss says, always put up a bravura front to the world, but he was a very human and sentimental man underneath it all. That didn't mean that Roxy couldn't be hard to please in the area of music.

"He would conduct the orchestra on occasion," Earle smiles. "His *pièce de résistance* was the 'Southern Rhapsody,' a medley of southern airs treated in a semi-symphonic manner by the compiler, Lucius Hosmer. I doubt if Roxy knew one note from another, but you would never have suspected that he was anything except an accomplished conductor. His performance was polished and highly dramatic.

"He always had his eye on showmanship in everything, even a mere cymbal crash. Once the orchestra was rehearsing the overture at the dress rehearsal and it came to the point where a cymbal crash was indicated. The man on the cymbals played it perfectly, but Roxy was not impressed. He jumped up from his director's table a few rows back from the orchestra pit shouting, 'Hold it! Hold it, Erno!' Vaulting over the railing of the pit, he took the cymbals from the musician and said, 'Erno, take it back a few bars from the cymbal crash. I wish to show this gentleman how a cymbal crash should be done.' The music started again and when Mr. Rapee gave Roxy his cue, he responded with a grandiose sweep of the cymbals that was both earsplitting and eye-filling. Then, returning the cymbals to the player, he said, 'If you don't mind, that is the way I would like to have it done. You see, when you played that crash before it was only a note in the music. Doing it my way, it becomes an event!' All of the percussionists must have been impressed because they continued to use that technique long after Roxy had left the Music Hall.

"Personally, I only had one run-in with Roxy when he was at the Music Hall. I had constructed an overture of some of the fast-moving pop tunes of the day. I had spent a lot of time on it and I thought I had done a good job. Being a great admirer of George Gershwin, I had borrowed a few of his modern chords to use in my arrangement because I thought they would help to make the whole thing more salable to the listeners. Roxy thought otherwise.

"Roxy hadn't heard the overture until dress rehearsal. I was sitting in the back of the house when it was first played. Mr. Rapee was out on a concert tour and Jules Silver was conducting the orchestra. When the overture was finished, Roxy got on his microphone and said, 'Jules, who wrote that overture?' 'It was scored by Earle Moss, sir,' Jules answered. Naturally, since I thought it was pretty good, I was expecting a compliment. But Roxy said, 'Well, he ought to be ashamed of himself. That is the *worst* overture of its kind I have ever heard. It's full of wrong notes!'

"Roxy was from the old school and he did not accept the newer chords as chords at all. He considered them *dischords*. Jules was nice enough to go to bat for me and told Roxy, 'Mr. Rothafel, there is not even *one* wrong note in this overture. Every note is correct.' Roxy then said, 'Don't try to tell me that I don't know a wrong note when I hear one. That piece is full of clinkers!'

"There was no time to change anything so Roxy decided to leave it in for the first show. I was highly incensed that Roxy's lack of musical knowledge had managed to humiliate me in front of everyone, so I stormed out to my favorite bar and indulged myself in a few noggins of Scotch and soda. By the time I had left the bar I was determined to tell Roxy in a few well-chosen and obscene words exactly what he could do with his job if he made any more unjust remarks about my overture.

"It was the custom to hold a production meeting up in the large rehearsal hall after each opening performance. The entire company would attend to learn what changes, if any, would be made in the second show. I was there along with everyone else when Roxy came in, went to his table, and

The opera *Madame Butterfly* was the main stage attraction in this early 1930s
photo of the Music Hall. (Courtesy of the Bettmann Archive.)

Music Director Will Irwin studies old scores in the subbasement
music library at Radio City. (Courtesy of Bob Coogan.)

rapped for attention. 'All right,' he said, 'let's take it from the overture. Jules, who did you say wrote that score?' Jules reminded him of my name and Roxy stood up and said, 'Earle Moss, are you here?' I held my hand up to signify my presence and he said, 'Would you please come up here, Moss? I wish to talk to you.'

"I was certain that this was surely 'the moment of truth.' I was all ready to tell him off as I walked up to him. But he completely surprised me by stretching out his big hand and saying, 'Mr. Moss, I wish to congratulate you upon your fine workmanship. In all of my experience in show business, I have *never* heard a finer popular overture! It is great, really great, and I thank you for your fine job.' Well, I was so surprised and pleased that the mental chip I had been carrying on my shoulder fell right off. I shook his hand and thanked him for his kind words to the accompaniment of a smattering of applause from the assembled company. I had been vindicated.

"Confucius once wrote something that could be applied to Roxy. He wrote: 'The superior man is hard to please but easy to serve. The inferior man is easy to please but hard to serve.' That was also the case with Erno Rapee. He was hard to please, but if your work was satisfactory to him, he was very easy to work with."

John Dosso has served longest on the Radio City music staff. By 1978 he had limited his activities to that of music librarian, looking after a collection estimated to be worth at least two million dollars. Dosso works in a huge room some two and a half floors below street level. The room is crammed to the ceiling with file cabinets containing every piece of music ever heard in the Music Hall since 1932. He first came to the theater in 1937 and was an associate conductor for nearly twenty-five years. He has worked with every one of the musical directors since the Music Hall opened.

Dosso also speaks of Erno Rapee with special fondness and considers his loss one of the greatest the Music Hall has ever suffered. "As I recall," he says, "I had conducted the first three shows of the day and Erno was scheduled to do the final performance. I went to his dressing room to say goodnight and he said 'I'll see you tomorrow.' Next morning I heard that he was dead."

Dosso remembers the era when it was standard practice for the Music Hall to stage "tab" versions of operas as part of the daily bill. In one instance, many years ago, the Music Hall arrangers had to condense the opera *Madame Butterfly* from its normal running time of two to two and a half hours down to one hour. The opera, featuring Jan Peerce and others, was presented on the Music Hall stage four times a day. Peerce and the other leads would usually sing two performances a day, while their alternates would go on for the other two shows.

There are only a handful of orchestra members today who have been at the Music Hall for twenty-five years or more. Many of them, tiring of the hectic schedule of four or five performances a day, went on to perform with the Philharmonic and the Metropolitan Opera or other orchestras where the pace wasn't so hectic.

Charles Previn, who had worked for Roxy at the Roxy Theatre, and had joined him at the Music Hall as an associate conductor, took over the musical directorship when Rapee died. Previn was followed by Alexander Smallens, who was eventually replaced by Raymond Paige. Paige immediately became one of the most controversial and celebrated conductors in Music Hall history. He took it upon himself to revamp the entire music department. In the early days, the Musician's Union was not as tough in its contracts as it is today, and Paige was able to "fire almost half the orchestra before anybody knew what was happening." He replaced many of the Music Hall's old-timers with musicians and staff people of his own choosing and headed the music department during the theater's most financially successful period.

Paige and Leon Leonidoff were both extremely strong-willed individualists and the conductor and the senior producer reportedly had many heated battles during rehearsals. On one occasion, after a lengthy argument with Paige in front of the assembled company, Leonidoff threw up his hands in disgust and shouted "Raymond, when two people are saying the same thing . . . one of them has to be wrong!"

After Paige's death in 1963, Will Irwin and Rayburn Wright, both associate conductors and orchestrators, shared the podium and the director's job until the end of the decade. Paul Lavalle was then brought in as musical director. Lavalle's reign was brief and stormy, and Irwin was soon reinstated as sole director and continued on in that capacity through the seventies.

Irwin, primarily a legitimate theater conductor, decided to join the Music Hall staff in 1960 when he felt he had had "enough of the road." His theatrical career began in 1932 with Broadway's *Of Thee I Sing.* Many shows later he became musical director of the Richard Rodgers organization and was the New York conductor of *Oklahoma.* He also toured with the National companies of *The King and I, South Pacific,* and others.

Irwin has seen the Music Hall Symphony Orchestra shrink in size over the years, although he insists the quality has not weakened. He recalls that the 1932 orchestra probably numbered one hundred people. That figure was cut to eighty, then fifty-five, then fifty. Today's normal complement is between thirty-five and forty musicians.

The musician's contract in force during 1978 sets a minimum of forty pieces for the orchestra, but Irwin points out that when a member retires or seeks work elsewhere the Music Hall is not obligated to replace him. The 1978 Symphony Orchestra organization table shows a complement of eight first violins, six second violins, three violas, four cellos, and two bass. In the woodwind section are one legitimate flute and one legitimate clarinet plus a first oboe player who doubles on first tenor saxophone, a second oboe player who doubles on second alto saxophone and English horn, a second clarinet player who doubles on first alto saxophone and bass clarinet, a first bassoon player who doubles on second tenor saxophone, and a second bassoon player who doubles on baritone saxophone. The orchestra is rounded out by two legitimate trombones, three trumpets, three trombones, a tuba, two percussionists, piano, and harp.

Irwin explains that while the orchestra has grown smaller, the musical director's duties have increased over the years. Long gone are the staffs of arrangers and composers. Irwin is his own staff composer and arranger. He is quick to point out that he hires James Timmons on a "per-job basis" to aid him with the arrangements, and brings in Luther Henderson from time to time for similar duties.

As in the case of the Rockettes, the Symphony Orchestra rehearsals are dependent upon the run of the feature film. Irwin starts planning the music for the next show immediately after the current show is on the boards. He meets with Rockette Director Violet Holmes and her arranger Don Smith to work out the music for the Rockettes' routine. If a ballet number or other special act is scheduled, he must meet with those in charge well in advance to begin planning the music for those routines. He is also director of the chorus. Actual orchestra rehearsals traditionally begin on the Monday before the Thursday opening of a new show. The orchestra rehearses primarily in what was once the Music Hall's own broadcast and recording studios on an upper floor of the great complex of rooms surrounding the stage. (The recording room has been leased by the Music Hall to an outside recording company in recent years.) Musicians, unlike the Rockettes, work a five-day week and also have a complement of standby musicians to take their places on days off and vacation time.

The Glee Club, once a spectacular part of every Music Hall stage production, was the first regular performing body completely dropped from the staff in the mid-1950s. In its heyday, the Glee Club numbered at least thirty excellent voices including those of Metropolitan Opera stars Peerce, Weede, and Warren, mentioned earlier. Since that time, choral groups have been hired on a "per-show" basis. Normally, around ten singers are brought in for a show. On special occasions as many as sixteen

A close-up of the console of the "Mighty Wurlitzer" organ in its special niche in the northern wall of the auditorium. (Herbert Gehr, Life Magazine © 1942, Time, Inc.)

are used. Chorus members belong to the American Guild of Variety Artists and also work on Broadway shows when roles are available. In the old days, the Music Hall salaries were actually higher than those paid to chorus members on Broadway. In 1978 a Music Hall chorus member received approximately $265 per week, while the Broadway chorus minimum was $350.

Since late in 1970 when he did his first Music Hall show, tenor Joe McGrath has become almost a "regular" in the vocal department. His rich "Irish tenor" voice has graced the stage more than any other soloist in recent years. In 1976 McGrath performed as a soloist on the Great Stage for twenty-five consecutive weeks. McGrath also often doubles as master of ceremonies during the Music

Hall productions. Like all the other singers, he is also available for duty as an "actor" in crowd scenes, etc. McGrath points out that female singers are hired primarily for the Christmas and Easter shows where they can also double as "atmosphere" for the traditional pageants, where the stage is seemingly filled "with a cast of thousands." Soloists are entitled to private dressing rooms on the fifth floor on the Fifty-first Street side of the Music Hall, while chorus members have large "boys" and "girls" dressing rooms on the second and fourth floors, respectively, on the Fiftieth Street side of the building.

No examination of the music department at the "Showplace of America" could be complete without a thorough study of the "Mighty Wurlitzer." In an era when every movie palace, whatever its size, had to come equipped with an organ, Roxy ordered the biggest one of all built especially for the new Music Hall. It's been said that it would require an orchestra of at least three thousand pieces to reproduce the musical sound that one man can create at the console of the Music Hall's Wurlitzer.

The audience in fact sees only a tiny fraction of the great organ when the spotlight shines on the musician seated at his console on the left side of the auditorium. Like an iceberg, an immense portion of it remains out of sight. In fact, eight separate rooms were built solely to house the pipes of the organ. The metal and wooden pipes range in length from a whopping thirty-two feet to the size of an old-fashioned lead pencil. The eight rooms, or lofts, which house the pipes, are located on either side of the yawning proscenium opening.

These lofts are also remarkably engineered rooms that protect the sensitive organ pipes in addition to housing them. Both temperature and humidity inside the lofts must be strictly controlled. Cold air causes the pipes to go flat and hot air can make them sharp. Special machinery keeps the rooms moisture-free and the temperature never varies from between 72 and 75 degrees Fahrenheit.

The lofts also house the special instrumentation hardware of the huge organ. It is these ingenious devices that enable the organist to reproduce, almost exactly, the sounds of a xylophone, a marimba, a harp, a glockenspiel, a grand piano, tom-toms, trap drums, castanets, snare drums, military drums, bass drums, tambourines, cymbals, chimes, wood blocks, and all other manner of orchestral tools. Even the Music Hall's Symphony Orchestra does not come equipped with all of these varied instruments.

In a sense, the Music Hall organist is both musician and telephone operator. By pushing and pulling certain buttons, the organist sets into motion a complex set of electrical relays that automatically "dial" the proper sounds into play. Basically, the Music Hall Wurlitzer works on a principle similar to that of a telephone switchboard, although the results are startlingly different. By the same token, the Music Hall doesn't find it necessary to employ a muscular boy to pump the air for the organ as the church organists did in bygone days. The necessary air for the pipes is electrically supplied by a giant blower that contains some sixty separate fans.

The auditorium console was one of two installed in the Music Hall in 1932. Another console is located in the sound studio. Both consoles utilize the same set of pipes and can be played simultaneously or separately. Each weighs 5,700 pounds. In a final bit of concern for the comfort and convenience of the audience, the original designers created a system that automatically cleans and deodorizes the forced air that goes through the pipes to prevent any unpleasant odors from seeping into the auditorium.

In May of 1968 the Music Hall embarked on an experimental program of creating a new stage production every three weeks in an effort to bolster attendance. Musical Director Will Irwin expressed some reservations about the plan. Erno Rapee, with a large staff of assistant conductors, staff composers, and arrangers, was able to pull together a new show every week in 1933. Irwin had no such staff at his command in 1978. Still, he was smilingly confident the show would go on. The Radio City Music Hall Symphony Orchestra has never missed one since 1932.

TEN

America's First Permanent Corps de Ballet

In 1933 Roxy finally admitted to reporters that he was having some disagreement with the Music Hall Board of Directors over the matter of cutting the Corps de Ballet by 10 percent. The ballet company continued in the center of financial controversy until 1975, when it was completely dropped as a permanent entity on the Music Hall's performing roster.

To understand the true importance of the Music Hall's permanent ballet company, it is necessary to examine the position of that dance form at the time Radio City was built. Europe, of course, had taken the classical dance to its heart many years earlier. But in 1932, ballet was an almost unknown art form to the general American audience. To be sure, the great Pavlova and other European ballet companies attracted sizable crowds on their American tours. But there was simply no place in this country where an American ballet dancer could find steady employment.

For that reason, serious students of the dance today consider Roxy one of the true early friends of ballet and a prime mover in bringing it the recognition it has earned in today's "dance explosion." Purists can argue that ballet as practiced at the Roxy Theatre and the Music Hall can hardly be compared with the work of today's great American and European ballet companies. That is an easy argument to win. But remember that Roxy and his dance people were breaking new ground—actually introducing people to classical dance in a completely commercial environment.

Apparently Roxy had become intrigued by ballet at an early stage in his theatrical career. The Minnesota–Lower East Side–former marine included ballet acts in shows at his earlier movie palaces. When he opened the Roxy Theatre, the dance form grew to even more important stature in his stage productions. It was at the Roxy that he made a star of a beautiful young ballerina named Patricia Bowman. When he was ready to open the new Music Hall, a permanent ballet company was high on his list of priorities.

Roxy took Miss Bowman, his ballet director, and the nucleus of the company with him when he moved to the Music Hall. By so doing, he established the first permanent ballet company in America. Its director, Florence Rogge, is today a Music Hall legend. She served as director from the night the doors first opened in 1932 until her retirement in 1951. Miss Rogge was cut from the classical cloth of ballet directors. She was sensitive, creative, dedicated, and absolute master of every dancer she surveyed. Her longtime assistant and successor, Margaret Sande, describes Rogge's special talents.

"To me, Florence Rogge and Agnes De Mille had similar gifts. Each woman had an uncanny knack of looking at a dancer and immediately knowing how to handle them. I mean, each seemed to have an instinctive feeling of how to show a dancer off to his or her best advantage. Each had an almost business sense toward pulling out your best tricks and making you look good."

Again, the use of the word *tricks* is likely to put off the dance purists. But it should be remembered that "tricks of the trade" were a ballet staple in the days when ballet dancers were employed in the area of strictly commercial show business. In the 1920s and early 1930s, ballerinas who worked in vaudeville and Broadway musicals were usually given the mundane title of "Toedancer," whatever the extent of their classical training. In implementing Roxy's dictum to "uplift the public taste rather than pander to it," it was necessary to give the unsophisticated patron the spectacular in order to allow him time to appreciate the subtle.

For that reason, Rogge brought in soloists such as Harriet Hoctor, a great star of the *Ziegfeld Follies,* whose most spectacular "trick" was doing a low backbend while slowly revolving on her toes. Gloria Gilbert was another Music Hall hit in the early years. She had ball bearings installed in the tips of her toe shoes and dazzled the audience with her ability to spin with dizzying speed. Likewise, the adagio dance team of Myrtle and Pacaud were a particularly successful act with their astounding lifts and leaps as their silver-painted bodies glistened in the lights of the Music Hall's great stage.

But it was not all "tricks." Florence Rogge created the great ballet numbers that have been successfully revived to thrill succeeding generations of Music Hall patrons. The "Bolero" is perhaps the most famous and colorful of these dance spectaculars. In the early years a cast of eighty-six people participated in it, including the entire Corps de Ballet, all the Rockettes, the Glee Club, and as many as eight male and female ballet soloists. "Rhapsody in Blue" and the "Underseas Ballet" also utilize huge casts and have withstood the test of time in many revivals.

In 1932 the Music Hall Corps de Ballet was introduced in a schedule of two performances a day. Within two weeks that had been boosted to four shows a day with five on holidays. Margaret Sande recalls at least one occasion when six performances of the "Bolero" were danced in a single day. She also found the Music Hall stage "wonderful for spacing," but a spectacular problem in trying to fill its enormous depth and width.

Miss Sande got her first paying job as a ballerina at the Roxy Theatre. She was invited to join the permanent company at the Music Hall and was featured opposite Harald Kreutzberg in the symbolic ballet, "The Angel of Fate," on the opening bill. She left in 1933 to become half of a touring dance team and later went on to appear in a number of Broadway shows, including Moss Hart's first hit, As Thousands Cheer, and George M. Cohan's last show, I'd Rather Be Right.

She was on the West Coast in 1946 when she received a telegram from Rogge asking her to return to New York as assistant director of the Music Hall Ballet Company. When Rogge retired in 1951, Miss Sande became the director. As she remembers it, the ballet company and the Rockettes were approximately equal in number in the beginning. The number had been cut to a permanent troupe of twenty-eight ballerinas by the time she became director. By the late 1950s the numbers started to dwindle, usually with cuts of four girls at a time. When larger troupes were needed for particularly big ballets, other dancers would be "jobbed in." There had always been a history of bringing extra ballet dancers in for special shows. In the very early days, as many as four to eight male dancers would be hired to complement the permanent company. Sande remembers that several of these male dancers were classically trained former officers of the "White Russian" Army.

The Music Hall, in Sande's view, "would certainly have to be given its share of credit in furthering ballet in America. It was in the forefront of the movement long before Balanchine and the others." She admits that some of the Music Hall productions in the early 1930s were almost closer to a circus show than to a classical ballet, with the emphasis on more pirouettes, higher leaps, and more speed. But she insists that by the 1940s, "You had to know what was correct."

Even before the 1940s the Music Hall had introduced to its large public two dancers whose correctness in every classic detail have become even more appreciated through the years. The name Patricia Bowman, premiere danseuse, was emblazoned across the great Radio City marquee on the night of December 27, 1932. Before long it would be accompanied by another name of equal stature in the field of American classical dance—Paul Haakon. Both dancers have been retired for a number of years, but their artistry was remembered in special sections of the respected Dance Magazine. Miss Bowman's fully illustrated story appeared in 1976, and Haakon's in 1977.

Patricia Bowman was born in Washington, D.C., and began her studies at the age of ten. She made her professional debut in front of President and Mrs. Calvin Coolidge three years later in a Washington Opera Company production of Aida. But, true to the times, she was forced to turn to the Broadway stage for employment. She impressed the critics with her little solo in George White's Scandals, and used her new income to begin many years of arduous study with the legendary Fokine. Fokine would later refer to her technique as "absolutely flawless." She danced with Fokine's ballet company at the Lewisohn Stadium in New York, one of the few havens for ballet in the late 1920s, and continued to find paid employment in commercial theaters.

One of her partners at the time, Nicholas Daks, persuaded her to take an audition at the newly built Roxy Theatre. The occasion would prove to be a fortunate one with lasting effects for both Bowman and Daks. In time, both would move on to the Radio City Music Hall. The Roxy's Leon Leonidoff was impressed with the beautiful young dancer and brought her to the attention of S. L. "Roxy" Rothafel. What started as a one-week engagement grew into an association that proved to be the most influential of her professional life.

She made her debut at the Roxy Theatre in 1927 in a specially created number entitled "The Gold Music Box." With her partner, Daks, she made a spectacular impression on the audience and roused it to spontaneous applause during the course of the lighthearted number. She also made a favorable impression on Roxy, and vice versa. In later years she would admit that "she fell madly in love with him."

When Roxy gave his notice at the theater that bore his name, Patricia Bowman, Nicholas Daks, Florence Rogge, Margaret Sande, Leon Leonidoff, and the other creative giants at the Roxy followed the great showman to Radio City. At the Roxy she worked for a time with Massine and even went on a road tour of seventy one-night stands with "Roxy and His Gang" of radio fame. By the night the Music Hall opened, she had earned her star billing.

After Roxy returned to duty from his hospital sojourn in 1933, Patsy Bowman and the Music Hall Corps de Ballet reached a new height of perfection. Roxy's genius in the use of lighting and scenery plus his feel for the ballet "story," highlighted Bowman's flawless technique to perfection.

A 1936 monograph on Bowman by Walter Ware makes special mention of a truncated Music Hall presentation of "The Enchanted Bird" based on *La Sylphide* and presented by the Music Hall in 1933. Ware wrote: "This was unquestionably the crown of Patricia Bowman's achievement during her long association with Roxy. Founded on ballet in its most classical form, this *Sylphide* calls for no theatrical tricks; there are no successions of *fouettés*, no fast *pirouettes* or *grand jetés*. This ballet depends entirely upon mood and fluidity of movement abetted by a complete and perfect technical equipment. In this ballet Patricia Bowman was poetry itself." According to the distinguished dance critic, Bowman's artistry in that ballet at the Music Hall placed her firmly in the front rank of American exponents of the dance.

Patricia Bowman left the Music Hall in early fall of 1934 to star in a new version of the *Ziegfeld Follies*. It proved to be a tearful leave-taking because she was fully aware that the Music Hall, through the insistence of Roxy, had built its ballets around her. At the end of the *Follies* run, she appeared in another short-run Broadway show and made star appearances in specially choreographed ballet sequences at the Capitol Theatre in New York and the Paramount Theatre in Los Angeles. In December of 1935 she returned to the Radio City stage for the first of a number of special guest appearances. She remembers that "I'd always come back to the Music Hall in those early years."

Between 1935 and 1938, Bowman was a headliner in theaters in both Europe and America. She then entered the Mordkin Ballet as prima ballerina, and was later among those responsible for reorganizing that company into the renowned Ballet Theatre. Critics at the time, and since, have given her the ultimate honor of referring to her as "the American Pavlova."

Bowman's career was long and illustrious, and when the years forced her into retirement she turned to teaching. Although a beautiful woman with a long list of suitors, the ballerina had never married. She continued to live alone in her tidy West Side apartment. A tragic accident had left her with a broken pelvis that made dancing impossible and walking difficult. One day she received a telephone call from a man she had not seen for nearly forty years. The man was Albert E. Kaye, who had once commissioned her to choreograph and star in a ballet production of her own creation.

Ballet Mistress Florence Rogge rehearses the Corps de Ballet in the Music Hall's Grand Foyer in this 1942 photo. (Herbert Gehr, Life Magazine © 1942, Time, Inc.)

Widowed and lonely, Kaye had spent months trying to track down the whereabouts of the beautiful ballerina he had never forgotten. The old friendship quickly blossomed into romance and Patsy Bowman and Albert Kaye were married in February 1977. A complicated operation was completely successful in correcting her physical disability, and the Kayes now make their home in Las Vegas. That city, in early 1978, proclaimed an official Patricia Bowman Day to honor the ballerina's special contribution to American dance.

Like Patsy Bowman, Paul Haakon began his association with Samuel Rothafel at the Roxy Theatre. He was Bowman's steadiest partner at the Roxy and although not a member of the permanent company, was often brought into the new Music Hall to share the stage with her. Those who remember their early appearances together speak of them in reverential tones.

Haakon was born in Denmark, but was brought to California while still a small boy in an attempt to improve his health. He returned to Denmark after his California sojourn and broke all precedents by entering the ballet school of the Royal Opera in Copenhagen when he had passed his seventh birthday. His gifts were natural and he progressed with amazing speed. He returned to California within two years and managed to get an audition with the great Pavlova on one of her tours. Pavlova told him he was much too young and inexperienced to join her company but encouraged him to continue his studies and to see her again. The young Haakon saw Pavlova again in 1927 and was once more advised to "come back another time."

In the meantime, Haakon had the same problems every other aspiring ballet dancer of the period faced—how to continue to grow as a dancer, how to work, and how to "put bread on the

Patricia Bowman. Since her days at the Roxy and the Music Hall, she has come to be regarded as America's first important ballet star. (Courtesy of Rita Sears.)

Two of America's greatest early ballet stars, Patricia Bowman and Paul Haakon, in a *pas de deux* from the ballet *Scheherazade* on the Music Hall stage in the 1930s. (Courtesy of Orest Serglevsray.)

table.'' Young Paul began years of study with the celebrated Fokine in New York, and was rewarded in 1927 when the Maestro selected him to dance the difficult role of Harlequin in Fokine's romantic episode *Le Carnaval.* His success in that role gave the young dancer the courage to embark on a series of solo concerts. In 1930 he made a concert appearance at the Guild Theatre in New York, and was seen by Anton Dolin and invited to join the latter's company for an English tour. Fate came to his rescue and made reality of his oldest dream when Pavlova herself watched him perform with the Dolin group at a matinee in London. She immediately invited him to join her company and Haakon, at age seventeen, found himself as first soloist with one of the greatest ballerinas of all time.

The association became a tragically short one due to the untimely death of the great ballerina. But Haakon was finally in a position to get the attention he deserved despite his extreme youth. One European critic wrote: "The most enchanting number of the evening was a War Dance by the scarcely seventeen-year-old Paul Haakon . . . a light and agile dancer who, Pavlova herself has said, may become a second Nijinsky." Haakon's incredible elevation and ease with the difficult *entrechat dix* always prompted comparisons with the fabled Russian star. With the exception of Fokine, he became the only dancer of his time to perform the dramatic *Spectre de la Rose* made famous by Nijinsky.

Paul Haakon remembers his Music Hall days with a mixture of affection and relief. To him they were days of great fun and hard work. He made his first appearance there shortly after it opened, and he continued to come back for guest appearances until the early 1950s. He remembers the Music Hall rehearsal periods as backbreaking work. He would normally supply his own wardrobe, although the Music Hall costume department would create a wardrobe for him on special shows, necessitating his

wearing a mock-up of the special costume until dress rehearsal. Haakon would usually report to the Music Hall two weeks before the opening performance, and work (without pay) with only his partner and the choreographer until the entire Corps de Ballet was ready to begin regular rehearsals.

He's also proud of the fact that he never had an understudy at the Music Hall. "Actually," he smiles, "I did have an understudy once. I severely sprained my ankle during a strenuous rehearsal. They brought in a gentleman to replace me . . . I won't mention his name becaue he since has become very famous . . . but the understudy then proceeded to sprain his ankle. In the end I had to go on myself, all bandaged up. So, you see, I've never had an understudy go on for me."

Despite his international acclaim outside the Music Hall, Haakon always had to audition for Leonidoff and Rogge before every role he danced at the Showplace of the Nation. He considers the retirement of Florence Rogge "a great loss to the Music Hall." He still marvels at Rogge's ability to devise a new dance to more or less coincide with the theme of every motion picture that came into Radio City. And he praises the Music Hall as "the only place in the old days where you could see ballet on a year-round basis. With the few regular companies . . . it was spasmodic."

Haakon also has great praise for the Music Hall as a training ground for future ballet stars. In the early days, he says, it was the only outlet young dancers had for actually earning a living while they continued to grow in their profession. He points out that the most ambitious members of the Music Hall Corps de Ballet continued their studies and practice in the hours between their normal four shows a day at the great theater. Many of those same dancers later went on to regular ballet companies.

One such young ballerina rose to fame as the celebrated Melissa Hayden. Miss Hayden danced with the Music Hall Corps de Ballet for five and a half months during the 1944–1945 season. Florence Rogge recognized her talent and reluctantly agreed to let her break her contract when she was summoned to join Ballet Theatre. She later went back to the Music Hall as guest star during a four-week stint in the late 1950s.

Melissa Hayden says, "I remember those early Thursday morning dress rehearsals as great fun. I was absolutely delighted to get the job at the Music Hall. The place is a city unto itself. It taught all of us great discipline and certainly gave me a source of income which allowed me to stay in New York and study."

The study and hard work paid off for Melissa Hayden. Her tenure as premiere danseuse of the New York City Ballet brought her recognition as America's finest ballerina. In the late 1970s, after a stint at Skidmore College in Saratoga Springs, she opened her own dance studio in New York.

Margaret Sande says today that she feels the unions had a great deal to do with the eventual collapse of the Music Hall Ballet Company. While she is quick to defend the principles on which the performing unions were founded, she strongly resents the stringent work rules that she feels pose unnecessary restrictions on proper rehearsals. Before she retired, to be replaced by Bettina Rosay, she found it necessary to take unusual measures in order to rehearse the entire company. She would first work with the eight or so soloists, then send them on to a special rehearsal area to perfect the routines with her assistant. She, with the help of her ballet captain, would then concentrate on the entire corps before putting the complete number together.

By the spring of 1978 the remnants of the once proud Corps de Ballet were brought back to perform in a special number in the Easter show. The girls were costumed in heavy "bunny suits" for what amounted to a "vaudeville turn" having virtually nothing to do with classical ballet. For the young dancers inside those clumsy costumes, it seemed a sad note to conclude this brilliant chapter of Music Hall history.

ELEVEN

BACKSTAGE ARTISTS

A most important annex to the Radio City Music Hall, unknown to the general public, sits several miles away from it at the corner of 129th Street and Columbus Avenue in upper Manhattan. This building has no name and doesn't figure to be considered any time in the future as a potential historic landmark. It isn't heated in the winter or air-conditioned in the summer. This undistinguished three-storied building occupies about one half of a square block. Its importance to the Music Hall has increased as the years have rolled by and production costs have risen as dramatically as the price of beef and bacon, for this building houses nearly every piece of scenery used since the original opening night in 1932. From 1932 until mid-1978, the Music Hall had presented exactly 658 separate productions. All of the drops and set pieces used in those shows are stored in the old warehouse on 129th Street.

Behind the Rockettes, ballerinas, and other performers who grace those historic boards, are the art directors, costumers, lighting technicians, and others who furnish the inanimate trappings of glamour and excitement. Their work, while not receiving as much applause from the audience, is no less important than that of the performers who exhibit their talents in the glare of the spotlight.

The first art director at the Music Hall was Robert Edmund Jones. In his eagerness to make Radio City a totally new experience in the theater, Roxy wanted only the best. Jones, in 1932, was considered head and shoulders over any other American scenic designer. Even today theater experts hold Jones in the same awe that architectural critics hold Frank Lloyd Wright. Robert Edmund Jones was perhaps the greatest scenic designer in the history of the American theater. Yet he became the first casualty of that horrendous opening night at Radio City.

Studying his previous work in the theater, it's a wonder that Jones ever took on the job at Radio City. He was accustomed to creating massive settings that dictated the mood for serious stage works. Perhaps it was the extravagant salary Roxy offered him; perhaps it was the personal persuasiveness of the master showman; or perhaps Jones simply liked the challenge of trying something new in an impressive new theater. Whatever the reason, Jones took the job . . . and failed.

It seems likely now that the great designer's favorite project in the opening production was the set for the opera *Carmen*. Those who remember it say it was a masterful setting, rendered in earth tones to emphasize the underlying passion and violence that is *Carmen*. But they are also quick to tell you that the audience on that opening night came to see sequins rather than earth tones. Jones reportedly walked out of the Music Hall that night, disappointed with himself and disgusted with the production, never to return.

With Roxy hospitalized and Robert Edmund Jones gone, the Music Hall management once again raided the Roxy Theatre for one of the few great talents Roxy had not invited to join him at the new theater. Clark Robinson, a good friend of Roxy's, had worked with the showman at the Rialto and the Capitol theaters before joining him at the Roxy. Robinson seemed the proper replacement for Jones at the Music Hall. Although less than brilliant at design sketches, he was a master draftsman with such talent that he had more or less replaced Roxy as producer at the Roxy Theatre when the latter moved on to Radio City. Robinson resigned at the Roxy and brought his assistant, James Stewart Morcom, along with him.

The two designers immediately jumped into the work on the next production, which would be shorter, far less extravagant, and would feature the first movie ever shown at the Music Hall. Morcom, who did many of Robinson's sketches, would begin a career at the great theater that would cover a period of nearly forty years. Robinson, who had first risen to fame as the scenic designer for Irving Berlin's great Music Box Revues, would leave after six months.

Leon Leonidoff, who had already risen to a position of significant power during Roxy's illness, was instrumental in furthering the career of a bright and talented young man who had been working as the head costume designer. Vincente Minnelli, who would later achieve even greater fame as one of Hollywood's finest directors and the husband of Judy Garland and father of Liza Minnelli, became the Music Hall's third art director in its first year of operation. Minnelli's brilliance made his tenure in the post relatively brief. He was an intense young man who had visions of higher goals than the art directorship of a theater that had got off to such a shaky start. Minnelli's settings were both flamboyant and delicate, perfectly suiting the requirements for productions at the Music Hall. Art department veterans consider his sets for "Scheherazade" probably his finest work at the Music Hall. Unlike Robinson, Minnelli was more interested in the artistic sketches of the sets, and so brought in Bruno Maine as his assistant for the drafting plans. Maine replaced Minnelli when the latter resigned to become a Broadway director and designer and eventually move on to Hollywood.

Bruno Maine, considered by his contemporaries as more of a draftsman than a creative artist, began a career at the Music Hall that lasted for seventeen years. They were years that became more and more troubled for the sensitive designer. As Leonidoff's star rose, Maine's fell and the two fought continually. Eventually Maine became a heavy drinker and in a fit of anger vented his wrath on Leonidoff and the entire Music Hall staff. He was fired.

In July of 1950, Leonidoff approached James Morcom on the idea of becoming the new art director. Morcom, the former assistant art director and Minnelli's assistant, had eventually left the Music Hall to return as costume designer after World War II. At first, he refused the job. He had served three years as costume designer and was happy with his work. But Leonidoff's point that the art director's

An interior view of the packed uptown Manhattan storehouse where the Music Hall's scenery is kept. (Courtesy of Bob Coogan.)

Set pieces of scenery from old Music Hall productions in the storehouse. (Courtesy of Bob Coogan.)

job had more prestige and paid three times as much money won him over. Morcom became art director in mid-1950 and continued on in the position during the Music Hall's glory years until he retired in 1973. His twenty-three-year tenure in the post is the longest in Radio City history.

It was Morcom who personally selected the most recent of the great Music Hall art directors. Fearing that Leonidoff would bring in someone of lesser caliber, Morcom began grooming John William Keck for the job long before Keck himself was aware of the plan. Keck, regarded as America's best scenery painter, had been brought in for years to do the artwork on the most beautiful drops used at the Music Hall. Art directors on Broadway, at the Metropolitan Opera, and elsewhere heaped accolades upon the shoulders of the young artist who was more than content applying his brushwork on the outsized medium of stage scenery. But Morcom thought Keck the perfect man to replace him at the Music Hall and began something of an on-the-job training program in all aspects of art direction before informing Keck and the management of what he had in mind.

Keck, the son of sculptor Charles Keck who created the famous statue of Father Duffy in Times Square, nearly refused the job. Even now he says, "Today I'm just an art director. Then I was a star." Eventually, he accepted the position and remains in it to this writing. Now he hires the scenic painters from the Messmore-Damon Studios to do the jobs he once enjoyed. Chuck Gillette acts as his assistant.

Keck and Morcom, with a combined total of nearly thirty years of art directorship between them, say that expenses have become an increasing problem backstage at the Music Hall. The budgetary allowance for sets has simply not come close to matching the expanding costs. Even in the most successful days of the Music Hall, settings were budgeted at a cost of $5,500. That figure went on for thirty years until it was raised by a thousand dollars a few years ago. Whereas a forty-five- by ninety-foot drop might cost $500 during the 1950s, the same painted drop would cost upwards of $6,000 today.

Keck says, "One time I found one of the drops used in the opening bill in 1932. It was in the

Music Hall Art Director James Stewart Morcom poses in front of the working model of the Great Stage in this photograph from the early 1970s. The scale model stage has a turntable and three working elevators that all operate electrically. Morcom was the Music Hall's most prolific art director, in point of tenure, and also photographed most of the color production shots that grace these pages.

John William Keck, the Music Hall's current art director, works on sketches for the 1978 Easter production. (Courtesy of Bob Coogan.)

John Keck searches the uptown storehouse of the Music Hall for scenery that can be refurbished for a new production. (Courtesy of Bob Coogan.)

(MIDDLE, LEFT) Frank Spencer, the Music Hall's longtime costume designer. For a number of years, Spencer has also designed the sparkling outfits worn by many of the performers in the Ringling Brothers, Barnum & Bailey Circus. (Courtesy of Bob Coogan.)

This smiling gentleman, Albert Packard, is one of the real veterans of the great theater on the Avenue of the Americas. Packard has managed the business affairs of the Music Hall's costume department since the 1930s. (Courtesy of Bob Coogan.)

warehouse and I had thoughts of trying to refurbish it and use it in a new show. Just for the fun of it, I went through the files and looked up what it cost back in 1932. Would you believe it was valued back then at just $190? Today, one new drop like that could eat up the entire budget of a show."

Morcom, of course, was at the Music Hall in the days when a new show was produced each week. He says rising costs coupled with a budget that hasn't kept pace would make such a schedule impossible today. Every art director at the Music Hall gets the theme of the show from the producer, who would normally be considered the director in a Broadway show. The art director tries to keep one show ahead, beginning work on the sketches for a third show while the current show is being dismantled and a new one set up.

Historically, the Music Hall has never had as many stagehands and lighting men as are em-

ployed at the Met or on a Broadway musical. Normally, ten or eleven stagehands are used at the Music Hall. Some stagehands and electricians were dropped from the permanent roster in 1975, but they can be jobbed in for a special show if they are needed. Conversely, the Music Hall stage is so huge that the drops and large scenery must be built and painted elsewhere before being moved in the night before a new production opens. There is no place in the theater big enough to hold the sets except the stage, which is constantly in use. The Radio City prop shop, a huge area one level below the stage, is too small to hold all the stage effects, and the offstage scene docks must be utilized for the current show. The smaller set pieces are built in the Music Hall, and painters are hired by the day to do the decorating.

The aforementioned warehouse on 129th Street has become more and more important as the

(LEFT)
Leanne Mitchell checks the measurements on a Rockette costume for the Easter show of 1978. Miss Mitchell supervises the creation, from scratch, of every costume worn on the Music Hall stage. (Courtesy of Bob Coogan.)

Using Mimi Kingsley as a model, Music Hall hat designer Joe Stephan tests the functionality of a Rockette "horse-head" hat for the "Springtime Carrousel" production. Stephan's hats must not only be outlandishly attractive, but also light enough to allow the dancers to go through their strenuous paces. (Courtesy of Bob Coogan.)

costs of material and labor have risen over the years. It is not at all unusual for Keck to send his assistant along with a crew of stagehands to the warehouse in an attempt to unearth an appropriate drop or piece of scenery that can be refurbished and used in a new production, thus keeping the cost of the sets within the budget. Morcom and the other art directors did the same thing in their day. However, flooding inside the packed storehouse has rendered many of the pieces unusable and others may never be found because they're so buried it would be too time-consuming and costly to dig them out.

John Jackson is the current vice-president of backstage operations and oversees everything that transpires behind the contour curtain from labor relations to budgets. Jackson, with some thirty years experience in a variety of fields at the Music Hall, is considered by nearly all the employees to be the most indespensable man in the organization. Gone are the Leonidoffs and Markerts who were the real showmen who knew the stage and its operation. Only Jackson remains. Most creative people at Radio City today will say that the front office seems to care little about anything other than the budget. Reportedly, they seldom even express their opinions on the good points or shortcomings of any production.

Monetary problems have plagued every aspect of the Radio City operation. As an example, Costume Designer Frank Spencer reports that a Rockette costume for the opening show in 1932 cost $10 to create. The most lavish costumes for the principals on the opening bill went for $25. In the period between 1947 and 1950 when Morcom headed the costume department, a Rockette costume cost between $100 and $125. Today, Spencer must allot $300 to $350 for each outfit worn by Markert's high-kickers. While the prices for individual costumes have risen, the costume department has been cut back considerably. In the old days there were never fewer than forty seamstresses sewing away for the new show. In 1978 there were twelve.

Albert Packard, who was the manager of the costume department when the Music Hall opened, is still functioning in that job with Leanne Mitchell as his immediate superior. Every new costume used on the Music Hall stage is made in the eighth-floor costume department. By the same token, every hat or headdress worn by a performer is also created and made at the Music Hall in the hat department. Today's hat designer is Joe Stephen, who replaced longtime designer Andy Pelicano.

James Reynolds, one of the top men in his field, was the costume designer when the Music Hall opened. Like Robert Edmund Jones, Reynolds resigned immediately following the opening-night disaster. He was replaced by Vincente Minnelli, and Minnelli was in turn replaced by Marco Montedoro when Minnelli became art director. James Morcom took over the job in 1947 and turned it over to Frank Spencer in 1950 when he was named art director. Spencer designed all the costumes in the great days of the fifties and sixties and continues to do so to this day.

Jimmy Morcom, with years of service at the Music Hall as costume designer, assistant art director, and art director, still remembers his temporary duty in an altogether different capacity as the highlight of his Radio City career.

"It happened in 1933," he laughs. "Roxy had hired an actor to portray Jesus Christ in a 'Last Supper' tableau in the Easter Pageant. Well, I looked more like Jesus than this guy did. I became obsessed with this crazy idea and decided to go directly to Roxy. I told him I should play Jesus in the pageant during the five shows on the first Easter Sunday in the Music Hall. He looked at me for a bit, and then agreed. I did it that one Easter and had a fine time, although I was scared to death. You see, there was a spotlight directly behind my head to give me a halo effect and I was afraid the heat from it would cause me to pass out and you'd have 'Jesus' under the table at the Last Supper.

"Sometime later Roxy called me into his office and congratulated me on what he said was a fine job. He said, 'Here's a little something from me to help you remember your stage debut.' With that he handed me a five-dollar gold piece. They soon became illegal back then, but I kept it and I still have it. I call it my 'Jesus' money. It's my favorite keepsake."

TWELVE

...AND ON THE
SILVER SCREEN

Within a few years of the early 1933 decision to show feature films at the Radio City Music Hall, the great showplace on Fiftieth Street became the talk of the movie industry. It became—to the stars, directors, and studio chiefs of Hollywood—what Broadway's Palace Theatre had been to vaudevillians. It was universally accepted as the perfect launching pad for the eventual worldwide success of a big new film.

A careful study of the films exhibited at the Music Hall since 1933 (see Appendix for complete listing) provides not only an insight into the long-term success of the Music Hall, but also a quick course in the history of the motion picture in America. The glory years of the Music Hall were also the golden years of the motion-picture industry.

Crtics through the years have found logical reasons for faulting the Music Hall as a variety house. The size of its mammoth auditorium tends to shrink individual performers, depriving patrons in the most distant seats of the intimacy and close contact needed for the proper enjoyment of stand-up comedians, magicians, and other single entertainers. With its huge screen, perfect sound system, unobstructed view, and widely spaced seats, the Great Hall remains without peer as a movie house.

Although he was publicly opposed to the showing of motion pictures in the new Music Hall, there is concrete evidence that Roxy was fully prepared to incorporate them into the format if the need arose. Perhaps at the insistence of his RKO–Rockefeller Center bosses, Roxy had given his approval for the installation of excellent motion-picture facilities long before the fateful opening night. With all the movie equipment on hand and ready to roll, it was a simple matter for the management to switch over to the movie–stage show policy on January 11, 1933.

Nonetheless, perhaps because it was deemed not that important when the theater was built, the Music Hall projection room is one of the more normal-sized areas of the building. Still, it is large enough for the 1978 projectionists to quip that it is "nearly as big as some of those shopping mall cracker boxes they call theaters today!" It certainly is as large and as well-equipped as any projection room in America.

There are four projection machines in the main booth located at the very top of the auditorium's back wall. Each projector uses 180-amps of current, compared to the average machine, which utilizes 130-amps. At each side of the movie projectors are two large slide projectors for use in special events on either stage or screen. Much use has also been made of two rear projection machines installed in a special niche in the back wall of the stage. These machines are capable of creating wonderful action effects for the stage productions, although they have been put to relatively little use in recent years. In a normal year at the Music Hall, some 24,000,000 feet of film are run through all the machines.

The huge movie screen, like so many other things, was created especially for the Music Hall. The screen measures seventy feet wide and thirty-five feet high. Its vinyl plastic seams are electronically welded and its lenticular surface is coated in a pearlized finish.

The Music Hall was rather slow in adopting the curved screen necessary for the showing of CinemaScope or Cinerama pictures because of the confinement of the space in the permanent fly gallery over the stage. A suitable screen was finally installed in 1954 for the showing of *Knights of the Round Table*. The Music Hall screen is flameproof, sagproof, and crease-resistant. It is also treated with a substance that makes it impervious to heat, cold, and moisture.

In a situation where a shorter, taller, wider, or more narrow screen is needed for special film presentations, the one at the Music Hall can be radically altered by the projectionist in his booth 190 feet away. There are permanent borders on all four sides of the screen that either close in or open up by the press of a button that activates electrically operated regulators. The motion-picture sound system, high fidelity and stereophonic, is considered among the finest anywhere.

It was well toward the end of 1933 before the Music Hall chieftains fully realized the financial impact motion pictures could have on the big new theater. RKO's classic film *Little Women* was the first to be held over for more than a week. The Music Hall exhibited a total of forty-seven films in its first year and forty-three the next year. Several of those short-run 1933 films, including *The Private Life of Henry VIII* and *King Kong,* are now recognized as classics. *Kong* was the eighth movie to play the Music Hall and the management quickly saw its box office potential. But instead of extending its run at the Music Hall, they chose to run it simultaneously at the smaller RKO Roxy Theatre a block to the south. The first great "monster" movie played to packed houses totaling close to ten thousand seats per showing.

Still, the Music Hall did not begin operating in the black until 1935. Very few films were held over past the standard one-week run. In 1942 *Random Harvest* with Greer Garson proved to be popular enough to keep the stage performers out of the rehearsal halls for thirteen weeks. The theater's all-time film record was set in 1968 with the run of Neil Simon's *The Odd Couple*. The Walter Matthau-Jack Lemmon vehicle ran for fourteen weeks and grossed $3.1 million. Another Simon film, *The Sunshine Boys,* seriously challenged that record in 1975; and Simon's *Barefoot in the Park* grossed $2.3 million during a twelve-week run in 1971.

In addition to the aforementioned hits, a number of other films have enjoyed exceptionally long runs at the Music Hall: Cecil B. De Mille's epic *The Greatest Show on Earth* ran for eleven weeks and grossed over $1,300,300; *That Touch of Mink* took in $1,885,335 during a ten-week stay in 1962; Mario Lanza's *The Great Caruso* grossed nearly $1,400,000 in a ten-week run in 1951; Warner Brothers' *Fanny* enjoyed a run of nine weeks in 1961, grossing $1,573,580 during its stay; and *Mister Roberts* also played for nine weeks and took in $1,353,118 for its 1955 run.

Three movies lasted for a full eight weeks. *Ivanhoe, Seven Brides for Seven Brothers,* and *Sayonara* all played the Music Hall during the 1950s, with MGM's *Seven Brides* topping the other two in box office gross revenues.

The Music Hall management presented Cary Grant with an inscribed silver bowl in 1963 as a formal recognition of his significant contribution to the theater's success. Grant is the Music Hall's all-time box office champ. He has appeared in twenty-seven pictures, which have run a total of 113 weeks. Fred Astaire finished second in the Music Hall popularity stakes with sixteen films playing a total of sixty weeks.

Greer Garson's eleven films ran for a total of seventy-nine weeks at the Music Hall, for which the "Queen of the Radio City Music Hall" was presented with a jewelled gold coronet on the Great Stage. Twenty-three of Ginger Rogers' films have played the Music Hall for a combined fifty-five weeks. Katharine Hepburn's twenty-two RCMH movies make her a close runner-up to Rogers, although Hepburn's films ran for a more successful total of sixty-four weeks. Hepburn is the only performer, male or female, to have seventeen successive films open at the Music Hall.

Among directors, John Cromwell and Vincente Minnelli have been most successful at the Music Hall. Eighteen of Cromwell's movies played the Showplace of the Nation for a total of thirty-six weeks. Minnelli, who began his theatrical career in the design rooms of the Music Hall, directed seventeen films, which enjoyed a combined run of eighty-five weeks.

The Academy of Motion Picture Arts and Sciences was founded in time to hand out the first awards for film excellence during the 1927–1928 season. The Music Hall wasn't built until 1932 and its film product wasn't eligible for consideration until the awards presentation in 1934. An analysis of the Oscar winners and nominees in the categories of Best Picture, Best Actor, and Best Actress from 1934 until the present day fortifies the Music Hall's position as America's number-one movie theater.

Before 1944, the Motion Picture Academy nominated ten films each year for the Best Picture Award. The Music Hall had exhibited at least one of the nominated pictures each year until that date.

5.   "STAR OF MIDNIGHT"
Directed by Stephen Roberts
From the novel by Arthur Somers Roche
An RKO-Radio Picture
THE CAST

Clay Dalzell	WILLIAM POWELL
Donna Mantin	GINGER ROGERS
Kinland	Paul Kelly
Swayne	Gene Lockhart
Mr. Classon	Ralph Morgan
Tim Winthrop	Leslie Fenton
Doremus	J. Farrell MacDonald
Tommy Tennant	Russell Hopton
Mrs. Classon	Vivian Oakland
Abe Ohlman	Frank Reicher
Cleary	Robert Emmett O'Connor
Kinland Gangster	Francis McDonald
Corbett	Paul Hurst

Contour curtain made under the Ted Weidhass patents by Peter Clark, Inc.
Scenes and draperies built and painted by the Lee Lash Studios.
This Program Subject To Change Without Notice

(ABOVE) **Cover and inside of Music Hall program, including a little-known RKO film.**

(BELOW) **The design of the program had changed by the 1950s and '60s (Courtesy of Earle Moss.)**

In 1941 five of the ten films nominated for Best Picture had played the Music Hall; and four of the ten nominees in 1933 and 1940 had appeared there. The Music Hall exhibited three of the five nominees in 1950.

However, only seven of the more than 650 films that have played the Music Hall went on to win the Oscar as the Best Picture of the Year. The Music Hall came up with a winner in its first year of operation, although the film was not a "homegrown" product. The 20th Century Fox film *Cavalcade* had opened at New York's Gaiety Theatre on a two-a-day reserved seat basis. The film was an enormous success and the Music Hall broke its first-run-only policy and snapped it up for showing at the Music Hall at regular prices early in 1933. (That first-run policy would not be broken again until 1973.) *Cavalcade* won the 1933 Best Picture Oscar.

The film that neither Clark Gable nor Claudette Colbert were particularly eager to make titillated Music Hall audiences during a brief run in 1934. Frank Capra's *It Happened One Night* was named Best Picture of that year. The Music Hall couldn't claim another Best Picture statuette until 1938 when it exhibited Columbia's screen adaptation of the Broadway comedy hit *You Can't Take It with You*. *Rebecca* in 1940 and *Mrs. Miniver* in 1942 both debuted at the Music Hall and became Academy Award winners in the Best Picture category.

Although it hosted a number of nominated pictures including such excellent ones as *A Double Life, The Heiress, Father of the Bride,* and *Sunset Boulevard,* the Music Hall couldn't boast of another Oscar-winning picture for the next nine years. MGM's beautiful musical *An American in Paris,* starring Gene Kelly and Leslie Caron, opened at Radio City in the fall of 1951. It surprised nearly everyone by beating out the favorites, *A Streetcar Named Desire* and *A Place in the Sun,* for the 1951 Best Picture Award. The Music Hall's last first-run film to win an Oscar as Best Picture was Paramount's *The Greatest Show on Earth* in 1952.

Charles Laughton was the first Music Hall film star to win a Best Actor Oscar. He won for his portrayal of the bone-chomping, finger-licking, wife-shedding English king in *The Private Life of Henry VIII,* which played the Music Hall in 1933. Gable won his only Oscar in 1934 for *It Happened One Night.* Victor McLaglen made it three straight for the Music Hall when he accepted the 1935 Best Actor Award for his work in *The Informer.* Liam O'Flaherty's moving story of the struggle for Irish independence is widely considered among the best films of all time, but played the Music Hall for exactly one week.

James Stewart, Ronald Colman, Gregory Peck, and John Wayne all won Oscars for the Best Actor in pictures that bowed at the great theater on Fiftieth Street. Stewart won for *The Philadelphia Story* in 1940, Colman for *A Double Life* in 1947, Peck for *To Kill a Mockingbird* in 1962, and Wayne for *True Grit* in 1969.

Music Hall films have been most successful in producing winners in the Academy's Best Actress category. Eight actresses have won Oscars for performances in nine Music Hall movies. Diana Wynyard won for her work in the 1933 film *Cavalcade.* Claudette Colbert made it a clean sweep for *It Happened One Night* when she was named Best Actress in 1934. The 1934 battle for the Best Actress Oscar precipitated one of the biggest controversies in the history of the Academy Awards. Bette Davis, who had also graced the Music Hall screen in 1934 in *Of Human Bondage,* was not nominated for an Oscar. The resulting uproar caused the Academy to allow write-in votes for that category for the first and only time in its history, but Colbert was still the winner.

Bette Davis was named Best Actress for her portrayal of *Jezebel,* which played the Music Hall in 1938. Joan Fontaine won for *Suspicion* in 1941, and Greer Garson won the Oscar for her portrayal of *Mrs. Miniver,* which played Radio City for twelve weeks in 1942 (Ms. Garson's *Random Harvest* ran for thirteen weeks that same year). Two of Olivia De Havilland's Music Hall films earned Oscars for her—*To Each His*

Own (1946) and *The Heiress* (1949). One of the Music Hall's all-time box office stars, Audrey Hepburn, won for *Roman Holiday* in 1953, and Julie Andrews was handed her gold-plated, tin statuette for her performance in *Mary Poppins*, which premiered at the Music Hall in 1964.

The Academy Award winners only tell a part of the Music Hall movie story. Oscars, after all, are a product of the industry itself. The nominations and the final vote are often affected as much by studio power, promotion, and personal popularity as they are by excellence. Time is the most demanding judge. Since 1933, despite its "family theater" policy, the Radio City Music Hall has introduced dozens of pictures that have endured under the stress of time.

Since 1933 a succession of chief executive officers has sat in the Music Hall's mini-theater and auditioned many hundreds of films sent to them by distributors. In days past the Music Hall was the most sought-after premiere house in the country. A first showing at the Music Hall usually meant almost guaranteed success for a film elsewhere in the country. The distribution chief for one of the biggest studios told reporters in 1952 that he would prefer to have his new picture open at the Music Hall than at any other theater in the world. He went further by adding that he would be perfectly willing to hold back the release of a picture to the rest of the world if he could first be assured of a record-breaking run at Radio City. If a film had already been a hit at the Music Hall, the fact was prominently displayed in movie ads everywhere in America when the picture was ready to go into general distribution.

It was not at all uncommon, during the 1940s, 1950s, and early 1960s, to see lines of people stretched out for blocks inside the Rockefeller Center complex. They would wait for hours to get into

King Solomon's Mines brought Deborah Kerr, Stewart Granger, and an excellent African cast to the great screen of the Music Hall in 1950. (Courtesy of Earle Moss.)

(ABOVE) **An agile elephant performs on the Music Hall stage.** (Courtesy of Vito Torelli.)

(BELOW) **Performers ride an antique car across the Music Hall stage in a 1968 production.**
(Courtesy of Vito Torelli.)

Spanish dancers take the Music Hall stage
in a whirl of blazing colors in
these photographs of a 1970 production.
(Courtesy of Vito Torelli.)

(RIGHT)
A 1957 Russell Markert production featured lovely ladies emerging from the covers of magazines. (Courtesy of James Morcom.)

(FAR RIGHT)
A popular magazine was the inspiration for this Marc Platt production called "Top Hat" in 1963. (Courtesy of James Morcom.)

(BELOW)
Leon Leonidoff saluted the RCA Building's Rainbow Room in this 1961 "Summer Festival" production. (Courtesy of James Morcom.)

(PRECEDING PAGES)
John Keck's lighted arch frames
the thirty high-kicking
Rockettes in a 1978 production.
(Courtesy of James Morcom.)

(LEFT)
Rockette Joyce Dwyer
emerges from a champagne glass
during this 1970 show.
(Courtesy of Vito Torelli.)

(FAR LEFT)
Russell Markert had the Rockettes
confined to pink rocking
chairs at the start of this 1962
Marc Platt production.
(Courtesy of James Morcom.)

(BELOW)
One of the last shots of all
thirty-six Rockettes lined up on
the Great Stage, in 1974,
the year the line was
reduced to thirty.
(Courtesy of James Morcom.)

(LEFT)
A close-up view of the hard-working Rockettes
in an open formation during a 1968 routine.
(Courtesy of Vito Torelli.)

(BELOW)
The Rockette line marches smartly upstage in
their military uniforms and then gives the happy
audience a snappy salute in this production with a
military theme. (Courtesy of Vito Torelli.)

(FOLLOWING PAGES)
The ceiling lights and the curtain glow a ruby red
as a spotlight frames the conductor before the Music
Hall Symphony Orchestra. (Courtesy of Vito Torelli.)

(FOLLOWING PAGES INSERT)
The Music Hall Symphony Orchestra at stage level
in an overture for a production in the spring
of 1978. (Courtesy of Vito Torelli.)

(OPPOSITE PAGE)
Framed against two of the great arches that make up
the auditorium ceiling, the organist plays his customary
concert on the "Mighty Wurlitzer," before the
curtain rises on the main show. (Courtesy of Vito Torelli.)

(BELOW)
The Rockettes flash friendly smiles in front of the
Halloweenish James Morcom backdrop in this October 1955
production called "Golliwag." (Courtesy of James Morcom.)

The Finale of the Easter show in 1960 featured masses of tulips that sprouted mysteriously on the Music Hall stage. (Courtesy of James Morcom.)

the Music Hall. Many of them packed lunches in anticipation of the long wait, especially during the Christmas and Easter shows. New York City police estimated that close to ten thousand were waiting in line outside the theater on a morning during the Christmas season of 1951. The line had started forming shortly after dawn, hours before the doors were scheduled to open.

To be sure, not every film at the Music Hall has been a winner. Not even television's *Late, Late, Late Show* has dared to show such Radio City oldies-but-not-goodies as *Aggie Appleby, Maker of Men* (1933), *The Good Fairy* (1934), or *Mother Carey's Chickens* (1939). The Music Hall executives have made their share of wrong guesses. Relatively few of Humphrey Bogart's great films played the Music Hall. The Music Hall also refused to buy Ginger Rogers in a nondancing and nonsinging role. Thus her Oscar-winning acting in the 1940 film *Kitty Foyle* was one of her few performances that did not grace the Radio City screen.

By and large, the Music Hall also stayed away from Westerns, which "packed them in" at other movie houses until recent years. Still, the few that have played the Showplace of the Nation, including *Cimarron, The Westerner,* and *Shane,* have been among the best ever filmed.

The Music Hall has also missed out on a number of great pictures that debuted on a "road show" or reserved-seat policy. The Music Hall has always sold its tickets on a first-come-first-served basis except for seats in the First Mezzanine, which have been more expensive and reserved in advance since 1933. Two of the great "road show" pictures that skipped the Music Hall are *Around the World in Eighty Days* and *Gone with the Wind*.

Gone with the Wind eventually reached the Music Hall in 1975, becoming the first picture to do so after opening elsewhere since *Cavalcade* in 1933. *Mary Poppins* opened at the Music Hall at regular prices in 1964 before being released to the rest of the world on a reserved-seat basis. The Disney classic was brought back to the Music Hall in 1973 as a special salute to Walt Disney on his fiftieth anniversary in the business. Nineteen seventy-five marked the real beginning of the Music Hall's break with its longtime policy of showing only first-run films. In a special experiment in that year, the theater exhibited four great MGM rereleases: the aforementioned *GWTW, 2001: A Space Odyssey, Singin' in the Rain,* and *Doctor Zhivago*. In recent years the musical *1776, The Sting,* and Disney's *Fantasia* have also been reprised.

Even the impact of television in its early days was unable seriously to disrupt the public's love affair with the Radio City Music Hall. A 1962 New York newspaper article pointed out that the Music Hall seemed to be the only theater in America still drawing tremendous business. While other motion-picture houses of the period were having terrible trouble coaxing customers out of their homes and away from their TVs, the Showplace of the Nation had its customary long lines waiting to get into the theater. In 1962, when many theaters were closing because of bad business, some six million people attended shows at the Music Hall. During the 1960s, the Music Hall consistently doubled the combined attendance of the Empire State Building, the Statue of Liberty, and the United Nations Building.

But, during the late 1960s, America began to change and the movies felt obliged to reflect that change. Against the grim background of the war in Vietnam, America's youth began questioning all of the old values and standards. There was a new air of permissiveness in the land—what some called a sexual revolution among the young. The youth, those within the eighteen- to thirty-four-year-old age group, were the film industry's most faithful customers. The industry, badly damaged by the impact of television, decided to capitalize on the new trends—to give the public something they couldn't see on their home screens.

Coupled with this daring new approach to film-making was the continuing practice of cutting back on production that had started several years earlier, a practice that continues to this day. (As an example: The entire industry, in 1978, had completed or started only ninety feature films as of mid-

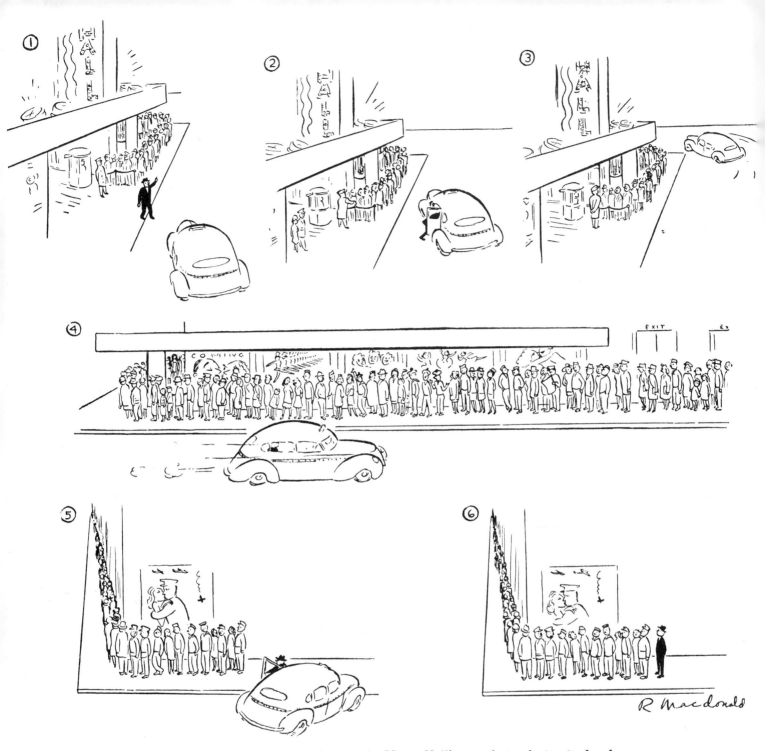

This *New Yorker* cartoon aptly depicts the Music Hall's popularity during its heyday. (Drawing by R. Macdonald; copyright © 1944, 1972 the New Yorker Magazine, Inc.)

July. The Music Hall alone exhibited more than half that number in its first year of operation.) The new Hollywood thinking began to have a strong impact on the Music Hall's box office. In 1971 James F. Gould, then Music Hall president, told reporters that he was not only worried about "the paucity of film product since the end of the 1960s," but was also deeply concerned about "the growing exploitation of raw sex and bad language in so many films." He added that he felt compelled to reject such films from his family-oriented theater.

Whether catering to the public taste (as the film-makers contend) or merely pandering to it (of which Roxy had accused the movie industry so many years earlier), there is no doubt that many of the new movies were either far too violent or sexually explicit for the Music Hall's conservative taste. The great theater of Fiftieth Street had built its reputation on clean, wholesome entertainment.

Still, a check of the list of Music Hall films of the past shows that the overwhelming majority of them had mature themes. Certainly *It Happened One Night, Sunset Boulevard,* and *Cat on a Hot Tin Roof,* among others, had subject matter as far removed from today's Disney fantasies as the blatantly pornographic *Deep Throat.* But the pictures of an earlier era chose to merely *imply* human sexual activity and other forms of nonpublic behavior rather than to *film* it.

The motion-picture industry was forced to reconsider its new policy following a loud outcry from religious and parent groups and others concerned with public morals and the possible effect the new movies might have on the young. Finally, in answer to the criticism, the industry came up with a rating system that would forewarn prospective patrons about the content of a new film. But the rating system backfired at the Radio City Music Hall.

The letters *G, PG, R,* and *X* immediately became more of a hindrance than a help to the fabled Showplace of the Nation. *G* was quickly recognized by most young adults as a symbol of dullness. And any letter lower down on the scale was a cause for immediate alarm to many parents with young children. The letters *PG,* after all, stand for *parental guidance suggested*—an admonition unnecessarily ominous in most instances. The family-oriented Music Hall found itself backed into a corner.

During the same period the movie companies began to experiment with new approaches to the distribution of feature films. In the past the big Hollywood studios were controlled by the Mayers and Goldwyns and Warners—men cut from the same cloth as Roxy—for whom entertainment was their only product. A first booking at the Music Hall was, to them, the most prestigious and desirable way to introduce a new film. But with more and more large conglomerates buying up the studios, the entire method of film distribution and exhibition began to change as drastically as the filmed subject matter.

The population flow away from the cities prompted the building of thousands of small theaters in suburban shopping centers. Mass "showcasings" or "four-wallings" were instituted in which the companies opened a new movie in dozens of small theaters in and around a city on the same day. The companies were able to save enormous sums of money on advertising costs by running a single large ad announcing the new film with the names of the exhibiting theaters in smaller print at the bottom of the display. Historically, the Music Hall has insisted that any film it exhibited could not be shown at the

Cast members salute Music Hall President James Gould (center) at his retirement party. His was the last financially successful stewardship of the "House That Roxy Built." (Courtesy of Columbia Pictures Industries, Inc.)

same time in any theater within a fifty-mile radius of Fiftieth Street and the Avenue of the Americas. The policy has proved to be a major stumbling block in its quest for new films of quality.

Its great size and tradition of playing a movie along with a stage show has also caused many distributors to shy away from the Music Hall in recent years. Figures released by Radio City in 1978 state that a minimum of $172,000 is required to keep the theater operating for a single week. That sum did not include film rental or real estate taxes. The huge overhead means the Music Hall can seldom offer more than a third of the grosses to a film booker. In smaller houses, with relatively minuscule operating costs, a distributor can earn as much as 75 percent of a movie's total grosses. Of course, that situation could change if the Music Hall booked shows that attracted capacity audiences as it did in days gone by.

The movies made the difference at the Music Hall in the early days, and the reason for today's box office slump can also be traced directly to the films being displayed on that 35- by 70-foot screen in Rockefeller Center. The two most obvious problems facing today's Music Hall film selectors are the fact that fewer films are being made, while those that are released come equipped with a label that prejudges their social value. Thus far the management has had little success in dealing with either problem, leaving the Music Hall's movie policy disastrously unexciting.

In its understandable desire to avoid anything that smacks of film prurience, the Music Hall had depended almost exclusively on films that carry the G rating. By 1978 the film fare at the Showplace of the Nation was rapidly transforming it into a "Kiddie Matinee" theater. The first six films of 1978 were: *Pete's Dragon* (a Disney picture with an animated beastie); *Crossed Swords* (the adventures of a very young prince and a pauper of the same age); *The Sea Gypsies* (a story of three young children who are shipwrecked); *Fantasia* (a rerun of Walt Disney's animated classic); *Matilda* (a dull tale about a boxing kangaroo); and *The Magic of Lassie* (the latest yarn about the collie of the 1943 film).

The movie versions of Neil Simon's Broadway comedies were the most successful in Music Hall history. Yet none of the prolific writer's new movies have been booked into the Music Hall since 1975, although they have proved to be successful without being shocking in any way. The tendency for the Music Hall scale to get stuck on G has been one of the reasons why the theater has missed out on many fine films that parents and children have viewed elsewhere, including the box office smashes *Star Wars* and *Close Encounters of the Third Kind*.

While the Music Hall was struggling with *Matilda* in July of 1978, generally accepted films of quality such as *The Cheap Detective, Capricorn One, Jaws 2, Grease,* and *Heaven Can Wait* (all with PG ratings) were doing excellent business in other theaters. (Ironically, the highly praised *Heaven Can Wait* was a new version of *Here Comes Mr. Jordan,* which was a very big movie at the Music Hall during the 1941 season.)

The Radio City Music Hall earned its reputation as the Showplace of the Nation for more than forty-six years. In addition to the brilliant stage productions of Roxy, Leonidoff, Markert, and others, it offered only the best feature films. It introduced us to the dynamic Bette Davis and the debonair Cary Grant. It was the first to make us familiar with the fragile strength of Katharine Hepburn and the grace and charm of Astaire and Rogers in film after film. It has been the queen of movie houses.

The intricacies of the rating system, "four-walling," distributor-theater percentage split, and all the other fine points of the movie business of the 1970s are difficult to grasp—but it is clear that their effect on Radio City has been nearly disastrous. The film industry once employed the slogan "Movies Are Better Than Ever" as a weapon against its biggest competition during the early days of television. That slogan will have to be actively implemented at the Music Hall if the familiar long lines are ever again to wend their way through the steel and limestone canyons of New York City's Rockefeller Center.

THIRTEEN

Gremlins in the Theater: Some Memorable Moments

A theater with a history of presenting a feature movie plus a live stage show a minimum of four times a day, seven days a week, fifty-two weeks a year for nearly fifty years must fall prey to "gremlins," no matter what precautions are taken. Accounts of these gaffes have become legend at the Music Hall and have been passed down from generation to generation.

With this in mind, ballerina Rose Novellino says she has always fantasized about writing a book entitled *Manure on My Mark*. She laughs when she explains the reasoning behind her "title." The vast Music Hall stage is covered with taped or painted marks that give the performers a point of reference for their positions during a show.

The Nativity Scene is the feature of the traditional Christmas show. Children in the audience are always delighted when assorted Rockettes and others disguised as shepherds lead in a procession of live animals ranging from camels to donkeys to goats to what-have-you. Trained in the basic rudiments of stagecraft, the animals nonetheless have not been "stage broken." As a result, the glamorous ballerinas and Rockettes must perform their intricate dance steps on a littered stage that would make a Manhattan gutter look sanitary.

One of the secrets of the Music Hall's longtime success is the sheer joy and exuberance its performers project across the footlights. The feeling is so infectious the entire audience usually becomes involved in it, sometimes to outrageous extremes. During the 1950s, one female member of the audience became so enthralled by it all she was determined to learn more about the inner workings of this happy troupe.

The woman was content to sit in her seat during the day's first stage show, but she apparently got up during the film and walked down the choral staircase until she made her way onstage. Backstage she wandered around, inspecting the equipment and visiting the various departments. She spent most of the day behind the scenes before somebody finally asked her business. Everyone concerned had assumed she was a new member of some other department.

From time to time, members of the audience feel the need to climb onstage and join the action. During the late 1960s a gentleman who had apparently had too many martinis before dinner or too many brandies afterward (or both), thought it might be fun to become an impromptu addition to the high-stepping antics of the Rockettes. The Rockettes, locked into their precision routine, could do nothing about the interloper.

Stage Manager John Denison was able to come to the rescue. With the cord from his earphones waving frantically in the breeze, Dennison stepped into the Rockettes' open formation, tried a few steps with them, hooked his arm through that of the wobbly patron's, executed a perfect "do-si-do," and danced the customer offstage . . . all in more-or-less perfect rhythm.

John Jackson, who by the late 1970s had risen to the post of producer and vice-president, started out as a member of the Glee Club in the very early years at the Music Hall before climbing the ladder from assistant stage manager, to stage manager, and eventually to his current position. Although he is now a deep-voiced gentleman with distinguished gray hair, Jackson starred in two of the most unusual Music Hall stories. Many years ago he was pressed into duty in front of the footlights when illness struck a featured act. The act, imported specially for that show, was a three-man juggling team from Switzerland. One of the jugglers had apparently eaten something that violently disagreed with him. Their turn was scheduled to last for eight minutes, and those precious minutes were desperately needed backstage to allow time for new scenery to be shifted into place for the next act. There was no way it could simply be dropped.

As a very young man, Jackson had been a performer, including a stint with a juggling act in vaudeville. With only minutes to go before the juggling act was due onstage, Jackson rehearsed the routine, struggled into the ailing performer's too-small costume, and went on. Reportedly, the audience never caught on to the last-minute substitution.

Jackson also used quick thinking to avoid another near-tragedy during the 1950s. The stage show at the time was one of Leon Leonidoff's massive spectaculars. Most massive and spectacular among the performers were three Indian elephants. They were, from the audience's point of view, the stars of the show. Shortly before the final performance of the first day, the trainer approached Jackson and told him he had a big problem. His elephants were hot and tired and he couldn't get them to obey. He was sure the reason for their surliness was a simple one—they hadn't had their daily baths.

Even the planners of the best-equipped stage in the world didn't have the foresight to install elephant bathtubs backstage at the Music Hall. Such eccentric appliances are generally hard to come by anywhere in Midtown Manhattan. Jackson, paying close attention to the trainer's warning that his elephants would not go on until they had their baths, sent stagehands scurrying frantically across town to the nearest hardware stores. They returned with garden hoses and scrub brushes in the nick of time, and the elephants agreed to go on after a quick shower, if not a leisurely bath.

Animals—camels, horses, donkeys, goats, sheep, dogs, and elephants—figure into a great deal of the legendary panic backstage at the Music Hall. If large animals can get into the act, so can small ones—like mice, for example. Joyce Dwyer, the current assistant captain of the Rockettes, has had a lifelong phobia about mice. She is absolutely petrified at the sight of one. A few years ago one of the people backstage decided it might be fun to play a practical joke on Joyce and possibly cure her of her mouse phobia at the same time.

Joyce, one of the shortest of the Rockettes, was chosen to stand inside a huge champagne glass for the production finale. Shortly before she climbed into her glass, somebody dropped a rubber mouse into the stem. Unaware of her unannounced traveling companion, Joyce climbed into the glass and was ready to be wheeled onstage. Suddenly she saw the mouse and, thinking it was real, began screaming hysterically. The stage manager yelled back at her, saying the curtain was about to open. True to Markert tradition, she swallowed her fear and posed prettily as she was wheeled on. She claims to be the only Rockette in history to perform with egg-sized goose bumps all over her body. But the show went on.

There has been cause for some real tension behind the scenes over the years. During World War II, government agents swept backstage at the Music Hall to break up one of the specialty acts hired for the show. One of the members of the team was wanted as a draft dodger.

The World War II draft hit hard at the theater's male employees. Music Hall old-timers swear that Leon Leonidoff was so frantic when he heard that one of his favorite regulars was going to be drafted, he tried to talk the draft board into letting the performer stay a civilian by offering them free passes to the upcoming show.

During the war years, the normal backstage routine was often interrupted by air raid drills. The performers all had assigned areas in which to flee possible hazard from falling bombs. One such area was the Grand Lounge. The drills didn't stop the Rockettes, in particular, from carrying on with whatever personal chores they had planned for between shows. One woman customer was startled to wander into the ladies' room in the Grand Lounge and find a Rockette using one of the sinks to wash her hair.

V-J Day, the end of World War II, was a riotously happy day at the Music Hall as it was everywhere else in America. The news came over a backstage radio on a hot August seventh in 1945. The show was in progress, but the news was too joyous to keep from the audience. An announcement of the Japanese surrender was made from the stage and the theater erupted into applause and spontane-

(LEFT) Cindy Peiffer (center) holds "Fred" the lamb as her sister Rockettes prepare to give him a bath backstage at Radio City. Fred was one of the more manageable animals to share the Great Stage with the famed precision dance troupe. (Courtesy of Douglas Herlihy.)

(RIGHT) The Rockettes greet Lassie and Jon Provost of the *Lassie* television show in the early 1960s. Lassie would make a return appearance to the Radio City stage in 1978. (Courtesy of Evelyn Ashley.)

ous dancing in the aisles. The Rockettes and other performers rushed into the streets to join the celebration as soon as their stage chores were finished.

Until recent years the Music Hall management was a firm believer in the old addage "the show must go on." Nothing was permitted to interfere with the policy of a minimum of four shows per day, seven days a week. But two events that traumatized the entire nation prompted a break with that long tradition. Franklin D. Roosevelt had been president-elect when the Music Hall opened, and continued to lead the nation through the dark days of the depression and World War II. With his sudden death in April of 1945, a special announcement was read to the full house at the Music Hall. The theater was immediately closed until the final evening performance.

The Music Hall program was interrupted again by the assassination of President John Fitzgerald Kennedy in November 1964. When the tragic announcement was made from the Great Stage, the stunned audience filed out of the theater barely able to believe the news of the loss of their young leader. The Music Hall was closed for a full day, and the Rockettes of the period remember watching the televised news of events surrounding the tragedy in their dressing rooms during every free moment for three days.

The Rockettes' dressing room television sets came as a personal gift from Russell Markert. In the early days of the Music Hall there was an almost endless variety of diversions to keep the performers and backstage people happy between shows—prompting the newsreel title "Music Hall Country Club." In those days there were some six hundred full-time employees at the Music Hall, and they were free to visit a special area on the roof for deck tennis, Ping-Pong, handball, shuffleboard, and numerous other sports activities. In addition, the performers had a special screening room where they could view new movies not on the regular bill. The films were supplied by distributors who hoped the Music Hall executives would select them for future exhibition at the great theater.

The Music Hall staff has always been a family affair in literal as well as figurative terms. Countless romances have started there and many have ended in marriage. At least one romance—between symphony orchestra trumpeter Norman Beatty and Rockette Claire McGuire—produced a second generation of Music Hall performers. Daughters Carol and Cathy Beatty now dance in the center of the Rockette line. Carol and Cathy are not the only sisters to be Rockettes at the same time, nor is their mother the first to produce future Rockettes. Millie Siller, a 1950s Rockette, proudly watched her daughter, Sandy, join the line in 1971. Sisters Irene and Sandy Summers, in the 1968 troupe, were among the other Rockette sister acts.

Two sets of twins have also matched high kicks on the Music Hall stage. Gloria and Grace Crystal were Rockettes in 1945, and Gladys and Edith Karen followed them into the line a few years later. Other areas of the Music Hall also have their family ties. Warren Jenkins, technical director of the theater, got the urge to join the staff at an early age because of the enthusiasm of his father who was a lighting man for Roxy when the Music Hall opened. Rockette Pam Kelleher has close family supervision when she performs. Her brother, Stephen, is the current assistant stage manager.

One of the backstage romances involved two veteran Music Hall performers who had been around since the 1932 opening. Earl Lippy became captain of the Men's Glee Club and took an interest in a beautiful young Rockette named Ginny Volmer. Ginny had been an original Roxyette and one of Russell Markert's earliest "dancing daughters." Markert "gave the bride away" at their wedding.

One of the most unusual shows ever presented at the Music Hall opened on April 5, 1962. It was unusual in many ways, including the fact that it was conceived and staged under the personal super-

American servicemen occupy many of the front seats in the packed auditorium in this photo from the World War II era. (Herbert Gehr, Life Magazine © 1942, Time, Inc.)

vision of Hollywood's Walt Disney. The production was called "Disneyland, U.S.A." and was billed as a special East Coast salute to the master cartoonist's sprawling West Coast amusement park.

Four huge van loads of theatrical properties were shipped cross-country to the Music Hall. There, in cooperation with the Music Hall technicians, a sizable portion of Disneyland was re-created on the Great Stage. Long before the Florida version of Disneyland was conceived, East Coast youngsters were able to come to Radio City and view more than reasonable facsimiles of the famed "Main Street," "Tomorrowland," "Frontierland," and "Fantasyland." They also watched thirty life-sized Disney characters including Mickey Mouse, Donald Duck, Goofy, Snow White and all Seven Dwarfs go through their antics onstage with the Rockettes and the regular show.

Disney also brought along a number of specialty acts from California to fill out the special show. The Marquis Chimps were on the bill as well as Balcombes in a comedy ladder act, comedian Wally Boag, banjo virtuoso Pat Theriault, and cancan dancer Graciella. The real highlight of the show was a barroom brawl staged by a number of Hollywood stunt men. It was a brief but altogether appropriate marriage: the West Coast's biggest family entertainment center joining hands with its counterpart in New York City.

It is interesting to note that the Radio City Music Hall, in its glory years, drew about six million people a year. At the time, all the Broadway shows combined were able to attract only about 20 percent more people each year. By the same token, a major-league baseball team today is deliriously happy when it can draw anything near two million people a year. When the Dodgers, Giants, and Yankees were all based in New York, the Music Hall consistently outdrew all of them combined.

Because of its vastness and longevity, the Radio City Music Hall provides a field day for trivia buffs. Consider this . . . it takes a staff of one hundred maintenance people to clean the theater every night after the closing show. In the early days, the staff was even larger. On the days when the World's Greatest Theater plays to full houses, two thousand ashtrays must be cleaned and a full twenty pounds of chewing gum must be removed from under the auditorium seats.

A number of the Music Hall staff have risen to celebrity status. Gregory Peck, who says he likes nothing better than watching a full house at a Music Hall performance, delights in telling the backstage people that he was once a guide in the great auditorium, although no actual records have been found that would prove or disprove the statement. Frank Little, a vice-president of the Public Broadcasting System, was certainly once a member of the ushering staff, as was Gavin MacLeod. MacLeod, who starred in the television shows *The Mary Tyler Moore Show* and *Love Boat*, cemented his Music Hall relationship by marrying Rockette Joan Rootvik.

From the very beginning, the ushering corps has been a very special element at the Music Hall. Roxy himself laid the groundwork for the stringent qualifications required to become an usher at Radio City. To Roxy, his "front-of-the-house" staff was every bit as important as the performers onstage. After all, it was the doormen and ushers with whom his paying customers would first come into contact. Their appearance and their manners had to be immaculate. Music Hall ushers were always expected to behave more like "officers and gentlemen" in the military sense than mere movie house ushers. That is one of the reasons the great showman had special holders installed on the walls near the entrances to the famed First Mezzanine reserved-seat section. The holders were there to display the name of the aisle usher. The practice has since been discontinued, although the name brackets remain.

One of the most famous of all Music Hall stories, absolutely factual, concerns an especially courteous member of the ushering corps. The other principals are a ballerina and an elderly woman the performers began to think of as "Mrs. Whitegloves." The woman was a Music Hall regular for several years and always tried to find a seat close to the stage where she could get a good look at the performers.

Looking like a well-drilled military platoon, the Music Hall ushers line up for morning inspection in this 1942 photograph. (Herbert Gehr, Life Magazine © 1942, Time, Inc.)

In time, the usher came to be better acquainted with the kindly old woman and always made sure she was given the best available seat. He found her immensely charming and genuinely appreciative of his extra attention. It should be pointed out that the Music Hall staff has always been forbidden to accept tips for their service, and the usher gave the woman special attention only because he liked her and had respect for her age. Eventually their relationship grew well beyond the bounds of common courtesy between usher and patron.

One day as they were chatting after the show, she asked him if there was any way at all she could get backstage to meet some of the performers. She was a devotee of the Corps de Ballet in general and of one young ballerina in particular. After some effort on his part, the usher finally got the official permission needed to take the woman backstage. She managed to charm the entire company and was obviously thrilled to meet her favorite ballerina in person. The ballerina also found her a lovable person and they became quite friendly over the months ahead. The woman was given the title "Mrs. Whitegloves" because she always waved hello to the performers with her white-gloved hands.

Suddenly, the elderly woman stopped coming to the Music Hall. The usher and the ballerina

Music Hall ushers carry their banner high during the Macy's Thanksgiving Day Parade of 1968. (Courtesy of Vito Torelli.)

worried about her absence, but had no way of contacting her to discover what caused it. Within a few months they were approached by the woman's lawyer. "Mrs. Whitegloves" had passed away. In reality she had been a wealthy widow whose greatest pleasure in her old age was to come to every new show at the Radio City Music Hall. She was grateful for the special kindness shown her by the usher and the ballerina, and she made a special bequest to them in her will. The usher and the ballerina divided a sum variously reported as between $150,000 and $250,000.

Needless to say, the Music Hall house managers have always used the story to remind the staff that kindness and courtesy sometimes pay unexpected dividends.

FOURTEEN

THE MUSIC HALL
IN DANGER

A message from the Rockefeller Center, Inc., management was tacked to the bulletin board backstage at the Music Hall on the night of January 4, 1978. The message said in essence that the entire company was "invited" to attend an important meeting at the Music Hall at 10:00 A.M., January 5, 1978.

The news leaked out well before Alton Marshall and Charles Hacker were able to tell their four hundred Rockettes, musicians, backstage workers, front-of-the-house employees, ushers, and others about it. Radio and television news programs and newspapers were full of the astonishing information. The Radio City Music Hall would be closed forever following the final performance of the Easter show on April 12, 1978.

It took no financial detective or mathematical wizard to come up with the reason for the closing announcement. It was all too obvious. The World's Greatest Theater had simply become a losing proposition. Audiences had been falling off each year; financial losses were increasing in direct proportion; and not even the powerful Rockefeller interests could afford to subsidize the place any longer. The figures released by Rockefeller Center President Alton Marshall were staggering. Rockefeller Center, Inc., had subsidized the hall for nearly ten years to the tune of an almost ten-million-dollar loss.

Hacker, executive vice-president of the Music Hall, pointed out that a weekly gross of $240,000 would be completely wiped out by the normal operating cost of the Music Hall plus the expense of film rental. And the great theater on the Avenue of the Americas hasn't been turning in weekly grosses of that magnitude on a regular basis for some time. According to the management, the rapid decline in business started in the late 1960s and escalated during the seventies. Between 1968 and 1972 the yearly income averaged close to ten million dollars. The annual figures dipped steadily thereafter to a low of $7.5 million in 1977. Hacker estimated that a full 1978 season would bring in no more than seven million dollars. In the opinion of the Rockefeller financial experts, the Music Hall operation in 1978 would cost the corporation close to three million dollars in losses.

Alton Marshall seemed adamant in his stand that the Music Hall must close. No amount of outside financial aid could save it. He called the World's Greatest Theater "no longer an economically viable entertainment entity."

It seems likely that Rockefeller Center, Inc., expected a considerable amount of protest over the decision to close the Music Hall, but it is unlikely that they were prepared for anything like the earthquake of protest that came pouring down upon their heads from all quarters. The news exploded in newspaper headlines across the country. Network television and national magazines took up the cause to save the Music Hall.

Within days *The New York Times* lead editorial concerned the possible loss of the grand old theater with a headline urging "Hold That Sunset at Radio City." Every New York newspaper as well as virtually every big city daily across the country took up the cry. *Newsweek* and *Time* magazines added their editorial voices. All of them made the same point: The Music Hall is unique in the world today. It is much more than just another old movie theater. It is a living museum of a classic period of modern design, architecture, and theatricality.

The Music Hall employees, without consulting management, decided to take the first step in fighting back. Over the dregs of cold coffee they decided the only weapon at their disposal was public opinion. They quickly formed the "Showpeople's Committee to Save the Music Hall." The New York Hilton Hotel gave them the use of an office, and they scrounged typewriters and a mimeograph machine and began printing petitions. In the weeks to come, the out-of-work dancers, singers, musicians, ushers, stagehands—in fact, the entire staff of the theater—would be combing the streets, making appearances on television and radio in an effort to rally public support to their aid.

Mary Anne Krupsak, New York State's energetic lieutenant governor, was the first public official to get actively involved in the fight to save the Music Hall. She told the Showpeople's Committee, "They'll close the Music Hall over my dead body!" Her later work proved she meant exactly what she said. New York's new mayor, Edward Koch, was quick to lend his vocal support to the fight. But he was equally quick to point out that he couldn't demand that any man stay in business when he was "losing so much money."

Money—or the lack of it—was the obvious problem. However, with only scant weeks until the April twelfth deadline . . . Time became equally important. Any scheme to keep the theater functioning would have to be carried off as quickly as possible. A way had to be found to blunt the Rockefeller bid to close the theater . . . to take the option away from them.

The only hope was to have the interior of Radio City Music Hall declared an official New York City Landmark Building. The ploy had worked in the past to save a number of historic buildings in America's greatest city. But time was the problem. Even if the Landmarks Preservation Commission could be persuaded to rush into a public hearing on the question, a final decision could take as long as two full months. Krupsak and others immediately went to work on the plan.

It was a painstaking process, but optimism grew as the weeks passed. If the New York Landmarks Preservation Commission would agree to meet, and if it voted favorably on the Music Hall question, other efforts could be made to proclaim it a National Landmark. In time the theater could become eligible for support from the National Endowment, the New York State Council on the Arts, and other arts foundations. As a Landmark Building it could conceivably be separated from the Rockefeller Center Corporation and operated on a nonprofit basis, letting that mighty organization off the financial hook and still keeping the theater for the people. The weeks dragged by until the good news was finally released: The Landmarks Commission would hear the Radio City case.

March had come in like a lion and the witnesses at the hearing were buffeted by strong, damp winds as they hurried up the City Hall steps. The interior of the second-floor hearing room was jammed with spectators. Marshall and Hacker were both in attendance and ready to testify.

The audience was obviously overwhelmingly in favor of landmark status for the Music Hall. Seventy witnesses spoke in favor of the designation. Only Marshall, Hacker, and three others spoke against the motion. Marshall, an affable white-haired gentleman, seemingly gained some sympathy from the audience when he related details of the staggering financial losses his corporation faced in trying to operate the Music Hall. But any feelings of sympathy quickly changed to raucous boos and jeers in response to one startling statement. With no preliminary buildup, Marshall warned that should the commission give the Music Hall official landmark status, he would "seek permission to demolish the structure the day after any landmark decision."

The statement clearly defined the battle lines inside the hearing room, although the faces of the commissioners remained unreadable. In the face of the vocal audience reaction, Marshall sought to ease his stand a bit. He suggested that he would be willing to enter into a written agreement whereby he would not touch the interior of the Music Hall for over 180 days without first consulting the Landmarks Commission. Of course, this was not the issue on that March day and the idea was not seriously considered.

Once the speakers against the landmark status had been heard, it was time for an interesting assortment of people to speak in favor of preserving the Music Hall. A group of kids from New York City Intermediate School 44 cheered the new speakers as loudly as they had booed Marshall. It was obvious in which direction their sentiments lay. One of the speakers was an elderly gentleman, "just a citizen," as he said. He suggested charging only a dollar admission for "old folks" who could help fill the theater during the afternoons.

Jack Kroll, senior editor for arts and theater at *Newsweek* magazine, testified that the response to his editorial urging that the Music Hall be saved "was absolutely unique in my experience. There was an overwhelming response . . . from all around the country." Other editors, from architecture magazines and periodicals, pleaded with the commission to grant the landmark status to save "a national treasure." Again and again, writers, museum curators, architects, designers, university professors, and other lovers of Radio City took their place in front of the microphone and gave compelling reasons why the Music Hall should escape the wrecking crew.

One of the people who testified in behalf of the landmark status spoke briefly, with quiet conviction toward the end of the long afternoon. She identified herself as an executive of the demolition company that would have the project of tearing down "The House That Roxy Built." She pleaded that some solution be found to save the theater, "because Mr. Marshall's loss is my gain. But I have the saddest job of all."

Art experts had come from as far away as Atlanta, Pittsburgh, and Cleveland to testify on behalf of the landmark status. But it was a gentleman from one of the farthest corners of the world who made one of the most moving statements. Arthur Lall, Indian Ambassador to the United Nations, spoke at length on what the Music Hall had meant to him, his family, and his countrymen who had enjoyed it on their visits to New York.

"New York," he concluded, "as a world capital, has a special duty to guard its great architectural treasures. You must remember it means so much to all of the people . . . not only of the U.S. . . . but also to the people of the world."

Joseph Papp, New York's most prolific theatrical producer of the 1970s, drew the biggest round of applause when he had concluded his testimony. Known for his innovative approaches, which have taken him from producing "free Shakespeare" in Central Park to an artistic association with the Lincoln Center for the Performing Arts to his own downtown theater complex to success in innumerable Broadway productions, Papp offered some suggestions on how the Music Hall could be put on a paying basis. But his most telling remark was brief and very much to the point.

Papp said, "When a theater gets into financial trouble you don't condemn the building . . . you condemn the management!"

The general feeling among the spectators in the hearing room was "if this were a criminal trial in a court of law, the Radio City Music Hall would go free and Marshall and Rockefeller Center, Inc., would be convicted."

But a Landmarks Preservation Commission hearing is not a court of law and, in this case, the "jury" deliberation takes weeks rather than hours. The commission did agree to make its decision as soon as possible—preferably before the April twelfth closing deadline. It would certainly waive its normal two-month period of deliberation in this special case. While the nation waited for that decision, the news media continued to play up the story as the "end of an era." After a two-month hiatus, the employees of the Music Hall had gone back to work in the 1978 Easter show. But many of them had already notified their landlords that they would have to give up their apartments in the middle of April.

There was a great resurgence of hope on March 29, 1978, when the newspaper headlines announced, "Music Hall a Landmark!" The Landmarks Preservation Commission had given the Music Hall official status as a Landmark Building. The first skirmish in the great battle had been won. Rockefeller Center, Inc., was legally prohibited from altering the interior of the Showplace of the Nation in any way for a period of one full year. Only a court battle could overturn that decision.

However, the forces trying to save the Music Hall were not in complete control of the situation. It was still Alton Marshall's privilege, if he wished, to lock the doors after the final performance on April twelfth and keep the great theater dark for a full year. There was no decree that he must continue the

Music Hall ballerinas in close-up during a 1968 production. (Courtesy of Vito Torelli.)

Gorgeously attired in eighteenth-century costumes, the Corps de Ballet and soloists perform in early 1968. (Courtesy of Vito Torelli.)

(OPPOSITE, TOP & BOTTOM)
The ballet company danced in the glare of a real neon sign
in the 1960 production of the Music Hall Follies.
The entire corps created a startling effect with their rhythmic
moving of ostrich fans in another portion of the ballet.
(Courtesy of James Morcom.)

One of the most famous and popular of all Music Hall productions is
the "Rhapsody in Blue," performed to the beautiful George Gershwin music.
This photo from the 1961 production shows the Corps de Ballet
beginning to warm to its task. (Courtesy of James Morcom.)

(ABOVE LEFT)
The lights have changed to blue as the prima ballerina begins her solo in Rhapsody in Blue. (Courtesy of James Morcom.)

(ABOVE RIGHT)
The Music Hall Corps de Ballet in a moment from the 1961 production of the haunting "Rhapsody in Blue." (Courtesy of James Morcom.)

(RIGHT)
The entire complement of ballerinas prostrate themselves on the Music Hall's stage turntable as the lovers stand triumphant in this finale from the "Rhapsody in Blue" of 1961. (Courtesy of James Morcom.)

(ABOVE)
The Rockettes augment the Corps de Ballet in this scene from the 1962
production of "Bolero." (Courtesy of James Morcom.)

(OPPOSITE TOP)
The world of Toulouse-Lautrec and bohemian Paris is re-created in this 1962
Russell Markert production of "Moulin Rouge." (Courtesy of James Morcom.)

(OPPOSITE BOTTOM)
The Rockettes are Parisian cancan girls in this 1958 Leon Leonidoff production
at the Music Hall. (Courtesy of James Morcom.)

(OPPOSITE TOP)
Classical ballet with a French theme in this 1962 production called "Carat."
(Courtesy of James Morcom.)

(OPPOSITE MIDDLE)
The Music Hall Corps de Ballet in costumes of the mysterious East in this Oriental ballet of 1960.
(Courtesy of James Morcom.)

(OPPOSITE BOTTOM)
An elaborate peacock setting by James Morcom sets the tone for this production
of the Oriental ballet in 1960. (Courtesy of James Morcom.)

(BELOW)
Whirling peasant costumes set the mood for this Music Hall ballet production in 1969.
(Courtesy of Vito Torelli.)

(ABOVE)
Grace and color mark the dancing and costumes in this 1968 Music Hall ballet.
(Courtesy of Vito Torelli.)

(RIGHT)
The entire company poses in front of Morcom's magnificent setting of
Russell Markert's 1960 Christmas show. (Courtesy of James Morcom.)

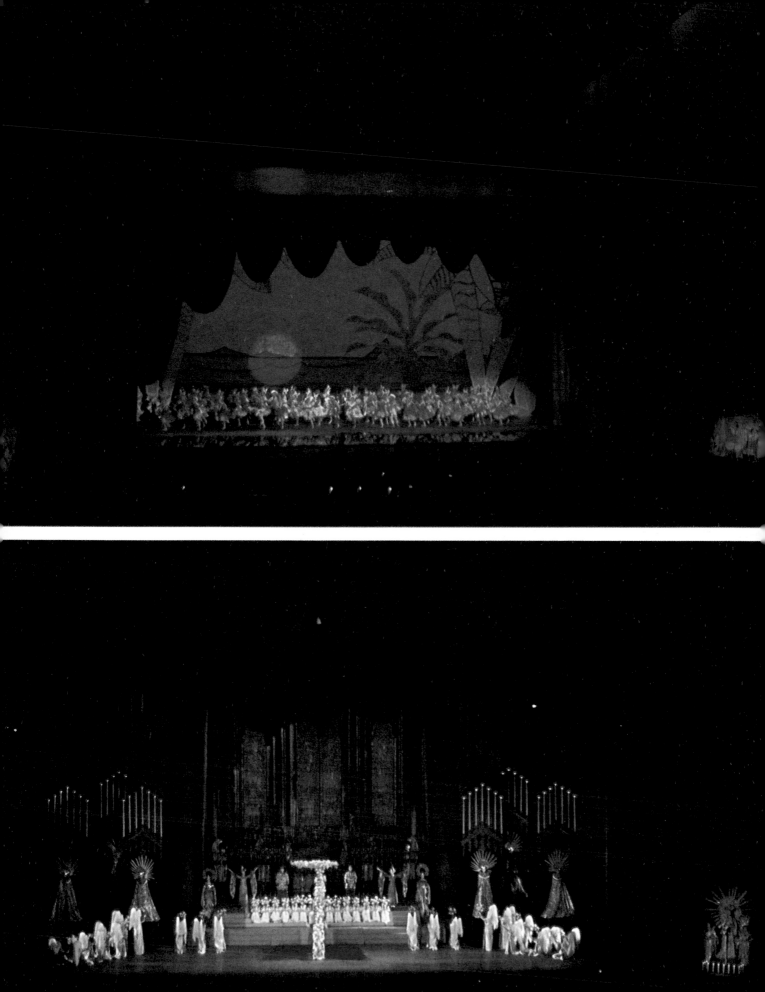

(OPPOSITE PAGE TOP)
A fiery tropical sun casts a glow on the assembled company in
the finale of the West Indies production at the Music Hall in 1960.
(Courtesy of James Morcom.)

(OPPOSITE PAGE BOTTOM)
The 1960 production of "The Glory of Easter." This medieval
pageant has long been an annual event at the Music Hall.
(Courtesy of James Morcom.)

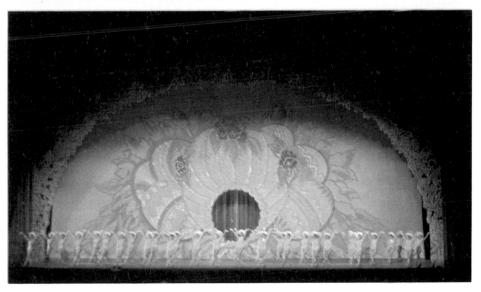

(TOP)
Following the majesty of the Easter Pageant, froth and frills are in order
for the Easter show of 1961. (Courtesy of James Morcom.)

(BOTTOM)
Bunny rabbits for the delighted children in the audience at
the 1961 Easter production. (Courtesy of James Morcom.)

(FOLLOWING PAGES)
Publicity shot for the recent (December 1978) NBC television special,
Rockette, starring Ann-Margret.

A
HOLIDAY
TRIBUTE
TO THE
RADIO CITY MUSIC HALL
STARRING
ANN-MARGRET

ROCKETTE

Thursday, Dec. 14,
9-11 pm (ET)
NBC-TV

A view of the Music Hall taken from across the Avenue of the Americas. (Courtesy of Vito Torelli.)

The Rockettes form a lineup outside New York City Hall before going inside to testify in favor of making the Radio City Music Hall a New York City Landmark Building in March of 1978. (Courtesy of Vito Torelli.)

New York's Lieutenant Governor Mary Anne Krupsak tries a tentative kick with the Rockettes on the steps of City Hall in Manhattan. (Courtesy of Vito Torelli.)

The self-described "heavy" in the Music Hall drama of early 1978—Alton Marshall, president of both Rockefeller Center, Inc., and the Radio City Music Hall. (Courtesy of Vito Torelli.)

Broadway Producer Joseph Papp minces no words in placing the blame for the Music Hall's declining box office receipts during his testimony before the Landmark Preservation Commission in early 1978. (Courtesy of Vito Torelli.)

Those fortunate enough to obtain tickets were given this program for the final scheduled performance at the Radio City Music Hall.

RADIO CITY MUSIC HALL
SHOWPLACE OF THE NATION IN THE HEART OF ROCKEFELLER CENTER

shows or allow the public to inspect the premises. But Lieutenant Governor Krupsak and others were determined not to let this happen.

As the days dwindled down, Marshall's position appeared to soften a little. At one point, with little more than a week to go, he told reporters he'd gladly turn the place over to anyone who could prove to him that it could "be operated without a loss." He added that he'd hand over the keys for a dollar a year rental if the Music Hall could be operated in a manner that would allow Rockefeller Center, Inc., to "break even" on its huge investment. However, he reaffirmed his position that there was no solution in sight to prevent the closing.

There was a tremendous flurry of excitement two days before the scheduled closing. The media trumpeted the story that New York State officials had worked out an agreement with the Music Hall management that would permit the building of an office tower over the theater. The profits from the rental units in the tower would then be used to keep the theater in operation. Mary Anne Krupsak and State Commerce Commissioner John Dyson were reportedly instrumental in arranging the settlement.

Within hours, Marshall emphatically denied the report. He admitted he had been engaged in discussion with a number of people about a variety of proposals. But he said absolutely nothing had been agreed upon that could possibly keep the Music Hall in operation. His position, he said, was unchanged.

The Radio City Music Hall would close forever following the final performance of the Easter Pageant on the night of April 12, 1978.

FIFTEEN

THE FINAL PERFORMANCE

Forty-five years, three months, and sixteen days had passed since the great Roxy ordered his uniformed staff to swing open the public doors of his huge new theater for the first time. In three hours or so, it would all be history. This would be more than just a night at the theater. This would be, at the very best, a deathbed vigil. It was the evening of April 12, 1978—the final performance, the closing night of the Radio City Music Hall.

There were some striking similarities between this audience and the one that had attended the opening in 1932. The celebrity-studded crowd began arriving early. Before the show they swarmed through all levels of the theater, looking long and lovingly at the Art Deco details of the grand old showplace. There were men in dinner jackets and women in evening gowns, and it's safe to assume there were representatives from nearly every state in the Union as well as visitors from abroad. It would be a packed house with tickets going from $5 to $25.

But there were also obvious differences. These people had not come to be the first to see something new and different. Nor had they come to stare at each other. They had made their way to this place to witness the death throes of an American tradition. They were patrons of the arts, 6,200 strong, openly paying their last respects to an institution that had become a part of their lives.

Many of the patrons seemed reluctant to take their seats. After all, they hadn't come out on this special night just to see a movie. Eventually, the seats were filled. The film, *Crossed Swords,* proved to be neither a great nor an offensive motion picture. It seemed to fit perfectly into the theater's policy of the 1970s.

In a sense, the movie symbolized what had happened to the Music Hall over the years. It was a remake of the old Mark Twain classic *The Prince and the Pauper,* which had starred the dashing Errol Flynn. The brooding muscularity of Oliver Reed could not begin to erase the memory of the twinkling eyes and debonair charm of the swashbuckling Flynn who played the role in the earlier version. Established box office stars Rex Harrison and Charlton Heston were relegated to so-called cameo roles in this new big-budget spin-off. Ironically, Raquel Welch nearly stole the show with her "bosom acting" . . . close-ups of her heaving mammaries expressing her supposed emotion without a line of dialogue. When she finally spoke, the audience burst into spontaneous applause.

The movie ended to relieved applause, and the recessed lamps in the curved ceiling bathed the auditorium in soft light. There wasn't an empty seat in the house. In fact, considerably more people than the official capacity were present. The upper reaches of the choral staircases that line the side walls were jammed with working press: television, newsreel, and still photographers. The moment was approaching.

The lights dimmed again and a spotlight picked up the musician seated at the world's largest theater organ. He played briefly while the stage was being readied for the Easter Pageant. When he had concluded, he was saluted with polite applause that began to swell in volume. It was as if the thousands had suddenly realized that this would be their last opportunity to show their appreciation for this man and his music.

A voice boomed over the loudspeaker system, raising a murmur of excitement within the huge audience. This was unexpected. "Ladies and Gentlemen, your host of the evening, WABC-TV's Stanley Siegel." The audience had not been advised beforehand of any extra performers or features. Could this be something to do with a surprise announcement that the Music Hall was going to be saved?

Siegel, host of a morning New York television talk show, quickly dashed those hopes. He explained that he had been asked to participate in the ceremonies for the host charity of the evening, the Variety Club Foundation of New York. He also told the audience that New York State officials were "at this moment" meeting with the officers of Rockefeller Center, Inc., in an attempt to work out a deal that would allow the Music Hall to stay open. He then introduced the spokesman for the Variety Club along with Charles Hacker, executive vice-president of the Music Hall. The Variety Club officer presented Hacker with a plaque honoring the Music Hall, and Hacker handed over a check to the Variety Club for $60,000, which represented the total proceeds for the final performance.

It was an ironic moment. The Rockefeller interests were closing the Showplace of the Nation because they could no longer *afford* to keep it open. Yet, on this final evening they were turning over the entire proceeds to charity.

The next feature on the program was also unexpected and a real crowd pleaser. The Music Hall's chief projectionist, Robert Endres, had pieced together a special film of Music Hall highlights down through the years. It began with shots of the opening night in 1932, followed the Rockettes to the 1937 Paris Exposition, and on to their USO shows for servicemen during World War II. The clips were faded and scratchy, but the reaction of the patrons was vigorous. The films only served to whet their appetites for the real thing—the last stage show ever at Radio City.

First came the annual Easter Pageant, "The Glory of Easter." It is probable that nearly every member of the audience had seen the spectacle before. Old-timers say it is basically the same pageant Roxy created for his Roxy Theatre before 1932. But, with the orchestra playing sonorously, the deep blue and red ceiling lights glowing overhead, the mammoth contour curtain rose on a scene that never fails to impress. The huge audience silently absorbed the scene as the spectacle unfolded, then applauded enthusiastically as it ended.

"Springtime Carrousel" was the title of the holiday stage show, featuring the Rockettes, Corps de Ballet, Chorus, and Symphony Orchestra. Its opening could have been taken from the 1930s or earlier, with an Irish tenor costumed in gray top hat and morning suit singing "Easter Parade" in front of an old-time olio curtain displaying "Easter Greetings." The ballet company, dressed in furry bunny suits rather than the traditional tutu and leotards, presented a series of numbers at the "Bunny Boutique." They stopped the show while dancing to the music of "There's No Business Like Show Business." The audience was quick to recognize there would be *no more* show business for these fine young dancers—at least, not in this theater. The Choral Group and orchestra also won hearty applause as they backed the ballerinas with their topical ballads. Eyes were already moist, but the best was yet to come.

More than six thousand voices roared their approval when the back curtains parted, revealing a gaily-festooned carnival set where the great cathedral had stood a few minutes earlier. In the rear center of the stage was a carrousel, slowly turning to the music of the Symphony Orchestra. The merry-go-round horses dipped and rose with the beat as the turntable moved on its axis. The horses were the thirty, bespangled Rockettes wearing high headdresses for manes and feathery flounces for tails.

The emotions of the audience overflowed again when the Rockettes descended from their carrousel and made their way to center stage. In an "open formation" they performed a unison tap dance routine to the music of "I Want to Be Happy." The audience caught the irony of the music and roared its approval once more. The Rockettes then made a maneuver never seen before. The line split in the center and the dancers worked their way toward the wings before sweeping forward onto a curving runway in front of the orchestra pit. The Rockettes were prepared to do their classic lineup almost in the laps of the audience.

The air was laden with figurative and literal electricity as hundreds of flashbulbs popped in an attempt to record this final moment. The theater exploded when the Rockettes went into their full line of eye-high unison kicks. This was always a show-stopper at the Music Hall, but no New York audience had ever reacted as this one did. The clamor started with the first kicks and built as the routine proceeded. The patrons were still applauding as each girl performed one last high kick and an individual bow until the end of the line was reached. The building rocked as the audience jumped to its feet for a standing ovation that lasted even after the Rockettes, some of them visibly shaken, had filed into the wings.

There was a grand finale featuring the entire company after which the performers were forced to come forward in answer to another standing ovation. The Rockettes moved onto the steps of the choral staircase while the audience continued to roar its approval, demanding more. In the most literal sense, "there was hardly a dry eye in the house" while the standing audience brutalized its palms and shouted itself hoarse. One man, clad in white top hat and tails, clambered onto the right side of the stage and handed the closest Rockettes bouquets of flowers. None of this had been rehearsed or expected.

The audience wanted more, but there was no more to give. Some of the Rockettes threw flowers back to the spectators. It was a love feast—and there were no more courses. The final standing ovation seemed to last nearly ten minutes. The performers, many of them openly weeping, made their way offstage. It was over.

There was no great rush for the exits when the house lights came on. The 6,200 spectators on the four levels of the Music Hall stood transfixed for a long, long moment. They stood with arms and hands aching from applause and eyes damp from tears. It was as if they couldn't accept what they knew to be true. There had been no surprise announcement. There had been no deus ex machina, no God Machine of the Greek tragedies, to provide this drama with a happy ending.

Groups of people clustered in front of the statue of "The Dancing Girl" in the Grand Lounge, closely examining the work they had previously taken for granted. Others posed for pictures in front of the staircases, mirrors, furniture, and murals that are among the precious treasures of the Music Hall. Large clusters of them lined the streets outside the entrances wanting to be a part of the closing-night scene. The great Music Hall wasn't completely cleared until nearly an hour after the final performer had left the stage.

The Rockefeller Center people (those not involved in the ongoing negotiations with the state of New York) made their way to a private get-together at a secret meeting place. Most of the Variety Club patrons and a host of celebrities attended a big bash at the Tower Suite restaurant across the Avenue of the Americas where they could look down and watch the lights go off on the Radio City marquee. The Rockette Alumnae Association had reserved a block of three hundred seats in the center section of the orchestra. They had their own party scheduled in a restaurant near the Music Hall. The current employees, those who had staged and performed in the final show, had other plans.

They had been offered a farewell party by the Music Hall management. It was to have been an informal "family" affair in one of the rehearsal studios. But they had rejected the offer, thinking they had no reason to celebrate the closing of what they thought of as their "second home." The same employees, after all, had formed the Showpeople's Committee to Save the Music Hall. They had fought hard to win their battle but had apparently lost. They chose to rent their own reception area off the Rainbow Room in the RCA Building and each paid $16.20 for a buffet and open bar.

No closing night in the theater is a joyous one for show folks; jobs are too hard to come by. But a closing night after a run of forty-five years is something else again. The room was a large and pleasant one, but it looked relatively forlorn and bare in the glare of the bright lights for television cameras. The media people were there in full complement. Some of the dancers, singers, musicians, and stagehands had sadly packed their gear after the show and headed home, sure only that they would be eligible for unemployment compensation in the morning.

But a considerable number of the employees put on their party finery and made it to the RCA

Building. Rockette Dee Dee Knapp was hustled in front of the live NBC News cameras the minute she entered the room. Two more Rockettes, Carol Harbich of Newark, New Jersey, and Pam Kelleher of Everett, Massachusetts, were directed to other open TV lenses. After the 11:30 news programs had gone off the air, things settled down to a quiet hum in the large room sixty-four floors above the city streets. The lights of New York surrounded the performers on every side of the RCA Building save that on which the Music Hall was located.

Only the open bar and the presence of the media kept things lively. In time, little groups of performers began to drift into corners of the room to discuss the situation. Inevitably, they all reached the same hopeful conclusion: "I just can't believe they're really going to close it!" From time to time, someone would tune up the room's public address system to announce, "There's no progress to report. The negotiations are still going on."

The sodden gloom of the aftermath of an exhilarating performance began to set in. More than an hour had passed and there was still no reason for the performers to expect good news. Later, at exactly twenty-three minutes past midnight, a new male voice was heard on the public-address system. Nearly two hours after the final curtain at the Music Hall, Stephen Kelleher, assistant stage manager, had something to say.

"Attention, all Music Hall employees," he boomed. "I have an important announcement."

The room was suddenly alive with a babble of excited voices and a rush of movement to the area where Kelleher stood.

"Attention, all Music Hall employees. All employees will report to work tomorrow morning, as usual. The Music Hall has been saved!"

The place erupted. The quiet gathering had turned into pandemonium with shouts of joy, applause, and impromptu dances choreographed by nobody. Reporters pushed through the crowd to get details of the settlement. None were forthcoming for several minutes until Rose Novellino, president of the Showpeople's Committee, took the microphone and announced that Lieutenant Governor Mary Anne Krupsak was on her way over with complete information.

Now it was a real party, even though the food and most of the drink had been depleted. Since January 5, the Music Hall employees and their party guests had fought the good, hard fight against overwhelming odds. And they had won!

Mary Anne Krupsak, looking more like a sporty suburban housewife than the sharp political infighter she really is, was escorted into the room by Rockette Eileen Collins some minutes later. She was greeted by a round of applause that rivaled that given the cast at the Music Hall earlier. She had got almost no sleep for three days, but she beamed her appreciation as she was smothered in hugs and kisses from the performers with whom she had worked for this moment. Finally she took the microphone and told the eager crowd that the Music Hall management had agreed to accept a proposal that would allow the theater to continue in operation for another full year. The Urban Development Corporation of the state of New York would invest as much as $2.2 million over the next year, and would also investigate ways to make the huge theater earn its own keep. The Rockettes and the Christmas and Easter shows would certainly continue, but she warned it might also be necessary to make some changes in the standard format. Most importantly, she promised to bring in a board of directors made up of show business professionals who would furnish up-to-date new ideas for the grand old hall.

The miracle had happened. The Radio City Music Hall would remain open at least until April 12, 1979. The wreckers' sledgehammer had been thwarted. The employees were ecstatic. But the more pessimistic members of the media were forced to wonder, "Are we starting the same process all over again? Will there be another crisis like this one year from tonight?"

Their pessimism was justified in just three weeks. Rockefeller Center President Alton Marshall startled everyone on May 3, 1978, by filing an application for permission to demolish the Music Hall. This application was filed exactly twenty-one days after Rockefeller Center, Inc., had agreed to the New York State plan to keep the theater functioning for at least another year. The move smacked of duplicity at the very least and brought another storm of protest from press and public.

A few days later Marshall backed off again saying he hadn't meant to give the public the wrong impression. He explained that the application to demolish was simply a technical move that would enable RCI to fight the Landmark designation legally, should the attempt to keep the theater operating without loss fail. Still, Marshall's $1,432 legal application already gave him the power to set into motion a complicated appeal procedure that would require additional hearings and action by the Landmarks Preservation Commission.

The New York State rescue plan was further attacked on May 11, 1978, when West Coast producer William Sargent filed a ten-million-dollar damage suit against Nelson Rockefeller, Rockefeller Center, Inc., and Mary Anne Krupsak. An angry Sargent told reporters he had made a handshake agreement with the Rockefeller interests in November of 1977 that would have permitted him to take over the Music Hall and transform it into a worldwide entertainment enterprise. He had planned to keep the theater intact for the presentation of nightly live shows that would have beamed around the world on closed-circuit television. He further charged that Rockefeller Center, Inc., had been misleading the public for a long time by pretending to have a real interest in saving the Music Hall. Sargent said the Rockefeller people's aim all along was to demolish the theater and build another office tower on the prime Midtown site. At the time of this writing the suit had not been settled.

The Landmarks Preservation Commission held a public hearing July 10, 1978, on the Rockefeller Center, Inc., application for a "Certificate of Appropriateness to demolish the Music Hall on ground of insufficient return pursuant to the city code." The RCI request was turned down by the Commission with only one dissenting vote. The dissenter noted that she did not favor the demolition of the theater, but was only expressing her opposition to the majority vote on procedural grounds. The report of the Landmarks Preservation Commission pointed out that RCI had the right to file again, without prejudice, at any time in the future.

At the time of the July hearing it seemed highly unlikely that the Music Hall box office would return 6 percent profit to Rockefeller Center, Inc. However, because of the furor of publicity, business at the theater took a decided upward turn during the first eight and a half months of 1978. The Music Hall drew 700,000 customers during the first eight weeks of 1978 compared to 1.8 million during the entire thirty-eight-week season of 1977. The film *Fantasia* did better business than expected and *The Magic of Lassie,* despite generally unfavorable reviews, proved to be one of the most popular Music Hall offerings in years. Much of the credit for its success was due to the stage show in which the canine star made four in-person appearances daily. *The Magic of Lassie,* playing only at the Music Hall, became the fourteenth top-grossing film in the nation by the end of August. That would seem to prove that the grand old New York theater is still capable of making a success out of a mediocre film without the aid of any "four-walling" techniques.

By the end of August it became apparent that the losses at the Music Hall would be only a fraction as great as those predicted by the management early in 1978. Perhaps because of that, Rockefeller Center, Inc., absolved the New York State Urban Development Corporation of its pledge to absorb up to $1.8 million in operating deficits. The move came as a surprise to most Music Hall observers. The management agreed to take over the entire operation of the Music Hall (although there were few outward signs that it had *ever* surrendered it) and promised to continue its "traditional entertainment format" at least until April of 1979. The UDC would continue its feasibility studies of means to put the Music Hall on a profitable basis. Marshall had reiterated during the July hearing that "I would lease the hall until 1994 to a non-profit corporation. Assuming that that released us from taxes, rental and all operating costs of the Music Hall."

One of the key ingredients of the April Music Hall–UDC agreement in principle was a study to build a tower over the existing Music Hall building. On September 5, 1978, word was leaked that the Urban Development Corporation was expected to recommend the construction of a thirty-one-story tower over the Music Hall. The new structure was expected to contain some nineteen floors of offices with the top twelve floors above the offices reserved for a new hotel. The Music Hall interior would not be affected except for some revisions in the ticket lobby where space would be made available for an entrance to the hotel. The full report on the new building was not expected to be released until the end of 1978.

The Music Hall stood to profit from other areas growing out of its association with the Urban Development Corporation. The UDC had made contractual committments to Guber, Ford, Gross Productions for several imported shows during the period when the regular Radio City performers were off. Frank Sinatra sang to sold-out houses for nightly performances from October 14 through October 27, 1978. About the same time singer Diana Ross also packed the huge house for her special appearances.

From all outward appearances the hiatus between September and November seemed likely to lower the theater's operating deficit considerably. Perhaps the greatest boon, from the point of added income and prestige, was the NBC television special utilizing the actual interior of the Music Hall. The two hour program, entitled *Rockette,* began taping on September 14, 1978, for an airing on December 14. The Rockettes joined Ann-Margret, portraying a Rockette, and an all-star cast including Gregory Peck, Alan King, Ben Vereen, Beverly Sills, Diahann Carroll, Greer Garson, and Jack Jones in a dramatized story concerning the performers at the Showplace of the Nation.

But even this seemingly-improved business outlook brought another swirl of controversy at the end of November. Richard Kahn, President of the UDC, predicted that the Radio City Music Hall would return a small operating profit by the end of 1978. Meanwhile, State Commerce Commissioner John Dyson criticized the UDC for voluntarily returning control of the theater to the Rockefeller Center Management. Dyson speculated that perhaps the UDC should have demanded payment from RCI before giving the theater back—"after we had demonstrated that the Hall could be operated at a profit." Kahn then dropped the bombshell that the UDC had no choice but to return the theater to Rockefeller control because the proper legislation to make the UDC the official tenant had never been enacted despite the April agreement.

The people who control the theater were quick to issue a rebuttal from their headquarters at 50 Rockefeller Plaza. The Rockefeller Center officials called the reports of a Music Hall profit for 1978 blatantly "erroneous." Admitting that the box office gross for the Sinatra and Ross appearances totaled more than $1.7 million, the RCI chieftains claimed that the Music Hall actually *lost* nearly $500,000 during the runs. Furthermore, the Rockefeller interests predicted that the theater would end the year with a "substantial loss." That prediction was based on their claim that the Music Hall had lost a total of $2.3 million during the first ten months of 1978.

In recent years the real-life story of the great theater on Fiftieth Street has read like a television soap opera with a new cliff-hanger every day. The Music Hall continues in serious financial difficulty and it is likely there will be more controversy and further legal hassles before these pages reach the printer. But the fact that a *building* can be in the center of an emotional storm only underlines its importance to us all.

The Radio City Music Hall has enriched our lives for nearly five decades. It has given us respite from our workaday worries through the Great Depression, three wars, and the terms of eight presidents of the United States. Roxy, in 1932, called the Music Hall a place of "magnitude and splendor heretofore undreamed of in the theater." The description still fits.

EPILOGUE

It should be apparent at this point that I have approached the subject matter within these pages with enthusiasm and affection. Like millions of others, I have had a long and loving relationship with the Radio City Music Hall. To me, it is a unique place that can never be replaced.

The Music Hall has become, in the closing years of the 1970s, a "traditional place to visit" rather than the exciting center of entertainment it was intended to be. We Music Hall lovers must realize that tradition, however laudable, should not be allowed to interfere unreasonably with enlightened self-interest in the operation of an enterprise so utterly dependent on the constantly changing tastes of the public. Tradition should not be allowed to keep the theater at arm's length from the public taste of the 1970s.

Those who control the Music Hall policy are to be applauded for their effort to keep the place as an entertainment center for the entire family. But have they succeeded in that goal? I think not. What they have done is present films, in particular, which would vaguely interest only the least sophisticated member of any family. Its recent film product has very little in common with that of its successful years when it did entertain the entire family. The Music Hall has gradually been transformed into a children's theater.

Certainly it makes sense to book fantasy films during the Christmas and Easter seasons. But what about the rest of the year? *Cue* magazine's William Wolf in his review of the Music Hall film *Matilda* (July, 1978) called it "too dull for children and too stupid for adults." He added, "The still-endangered Music Hall must have a death wish." I know of no dictionary that gives the word *insipid* as a synonym for nonprurient. An upgrading in film quality is desperately overdue at Radio City.

The stage shows have always given the Music Hall an extra dimension, but there is no reason why they also should not be more reflective of the 1970s than the 1930s. The talented Rockettes should be permitted to do new dance routines that relate to their own ages and the dance-crazed era in which they live. The traditional should be kept, by all means, but there is no reason to fear the addition of something new. Who could do it better?

I am in complete agreement with Joseph Papp's statement at the hearing of the Landmarks Preservation Commission: "When a theater gets into financial trouble you don't condemn the building . . . you condemn the management!" At this writing, the Radio City management is exactly as it was on April 12, 1978. The theater cannot prosper while this team holds the reins. Through benign neglect, well-intentioned incompetency, or whatever, its executive officers have allowed the World's Greatest Theater to drift to the brink of extinction.

As an example, the Music Hall officers gave me no cooperation whatsoever in the preparation of this book. My repeated requests for information and pictures were either refused or ignored. I was told, "We used to have a policy on that, but I'm not sure what it is now. I'll get back to you." I'm still waiting. I never received any kind of reply to my written request for an interview with the late Nelson Rockefeller. The Music Hall's official photographer says he was threatened with legal action if he released any photos without official permission.

Such shortsightedness in the area of promotion and publicity seems to be indicative of the general lackluster approach to the day-to-day operation of the theater by its executives. The Music Hall is desperately in need of another Roxy—a consummate showman with a burning desire to succeed.

At this point I have no inside information that would give me the confidence to predict the future of the Music Hall. Only one thing is certain to me. A remarkable theatrical institution like the Radio City Music Hall has a right to life—beyond the pages of this or any other book.

APPENDIX: RADIO CITY MUSIC HALL FILMS

The following is a complete list of feature films that have played the Radio City Music Hall from 1933 through July of 1978. The producing and/or distributing companies are listed in abbreviated form in parentheses following the film title.

1933 *The Bitter Tea of General Yen* (Col.); *The King's Vacation* (WB); *State Fair* (20th); *The Sign of the Cross* (Para.); *Topaze* (RKO); *The Great Jasper* (RKO); *Our Betters* (RKO); *King Kong* (RKO); *Christopher Strong* (RKO); *Sailor's Luck* (20th); *Sweepings* (RKO); *The Keyhole* (WB); *Cavalcade* (20th); *Working Man* (WB); *Zoo in Budapest* (20th); *The Silver Cord* (RKO); *The Warrior's Husband* (20th); *Adorable* (20th); *Elmer the Great* (WB); *Cocktail Hour* (Col.); *Ann Carver's Profession* (Col.); *I Loved You Yesterday* (20th); *Melody Cruise* (RKO); *Bed of Roses* (RKO); *Private Detective 62* (WB); *Professional Sweetheart* (RKO); *Double Harness* (RKO); *The Devil's in Love* (20th); *No Marriage Ties* (RKO); *Pilgrimage* (20th); *Morning Glory* (RKO); *Paddy the Next Best Thing* (20th); *One Man's Journey* (RKO); *Lady for a Day* (Col.); *The Power and the Glory* (20th); *My Weakness* (20th); *Ann Vickers* (RKO); *Doctor Bull* (20th); *The Private Life of Henry VIII* (Korda-UA); *Aggie Appleby, Maker of Men* (RKO); *Berkeley Square* (20th); *After Tonight* (RKO); *Only Yesterday* (Univ.); *Little Women* (RKO); *Counsellor at Law* (Univ.); *The Right to Romance* (RKO); and *Flying Down to Rio* (RKO).

1934 *If I Were Free* (RKO); *Man of Two Worlds* (RKO); *I Am Suzanne* (20th); *As Husbands Go* (20th); *Nana* (Goldwyn-UA); *Carolina* (20th); *It Happened One Night* (Col.); *David Harum* (20th); *Spitfire* (RKO); *George White's Scandals* (20th); *Bottoms Up* (20th); *Wild Cargo* (RKO); *This Man Is Mine* (RKO); *Stand Up and Cheer* (20th); *20th Century* (Col.); *Change of Heart* (20th); *Stingaree* (RKO); *Where Sinners Meet* (RKO); *Little Man, What Now?* (Univ.); *Sisters Under the Skin* (Col.); *The Life of Vergie Winters* (RKO); *Let's Try Again* (RKO); *Of Human Bondage* (RKO); *Whom the Gods Destroy* (Col.); *Grand Canary* (20th); *Hat, Coat and Glove* (RKO); *The World Moves On* (20th); *One More River* (Univ.); *The Cat's Paw* (20th); *The Fountain* (RKO); *One Night of Love* (Col.); *The Richest Girl in the World* (RKO); *Caravan* (20th); *Power* (Gaum-Brit); *Judge Priest* (20th); *The Age of Innocence* (RKO); *The Pursuit of Happiness* (Par.); *We Live Again* (Goldwyn-UA); *The Gay Divorcee* (RKO); *Broadway Bill* (Col.); *Music in the Air* (20th); *Bright Eyes* (20th); and *The Little Minister* (RKO).

1935 *Evergreen* (Gaum-Brit); *Romance in Manhattan* (RKO); *The Iron Duke* (Gaum-Brit); *The Good Fairy* (Univ.); *The Scarlet Pimpernel* (Korda-UA); *One More Spring* (20th); *The Whole Town's Talking* (Col.); *Roberta* (RKO); *The Little Colonel* (RKO); *Life Begins at 40* (20th); *Star of Midnight* (RKO); *Cardinal Richelieu* (UA); *The Scoundrel* (Par.); *The Informer* (RKO); *Break of Hearts* (RKO); *Escape Me Never* (UA); *Under the Pampas Moon* (20th); *Our Little Girl* (20th); *Becky Sharp* (RKO); *Love Me Forever* (Col.); *Ginger* (20th); *She* (RKO); *Curly Top* (20th); *The Farmer Takes a Wife* (20th); *Alice Adams* (RKO); *Top Hat* (RKO); *Steamboat Round the Bend* (20th); *She Married Her Boss* (Col.); *The Return of Peter Grimm* (RKO); *The Gay Deception* (20th); *Metropolitan* (20th); *A Feather in Her Hat* (Col.); *The Three Musketeers* (RKO); *Peter Ibbetson* (Par.); *The Man Who Broke the Bank at Monte Carlo* (20th); *Crime and Punishment* (Col.); *I Dream Too Much* (RKO); *In Person* (RKO); *The Littlest Rebel* (20th); and *Magnificent Obsession* (Univ.).

1936 *Sylvia Scarlett* (RKO); *Strike Me Pink* (Goldwyn-UA); *Next Time We Love* (Univ.); *The Petrified Forest* (WB); *Follow the Fleet* (RKO); *The Country Doctor* (20th); *Sutter's Gold* (Univ.); *Little Lord Fauntleroy* (Selznick-UA); *Mr. Deeds Goes to Town* (Col.); *Under Two Flags* (20th); *Show Boat* (Univ.); *The King Steps Out* (Col.); *Private Number* (20th); *Sins of Man* (20th); *The Poor Little Rich Girl* (20th); *The Bride Walks Out* (RKO); *The Green Pastures* (WB); *Mary of Scotland* (RKO); *My American Wife* (Par.); *Swing Time* (RKO); *My Man Godfrey* (Univ.); *Craig's Wife* (Col.); *The Gay Desperado* (UA); *Adventure in Manhattan* (Col.); *A Woman Rebels* (RKO); *As You Like It* (20th); *Theodora Goes Wild* (Col.); *The Garden of Allah* (Selznick-UA); *Winterset* (RKO); *More Than a Secretary* (RKO); *Rainbow on the River* (RKO); and *That Girl from Paris* (RKO).

1937 *Lloyds of London* (20th); *The Plough and the Stars* (RKO); *On the Avenue* (20th); *When You're in Love* (Col.); *Fire over England* (Korda-UA); *Wings of the Morning* (20th); *When's Your Birthday?* (RKO); *Seventh Heaven* (20th); *Quality Street* (RKO); *The Woman I Love* (RKO); *A Star Is Born* (Selznick-UA); *Shall We Dance* (RKO); *This Is My Affair* (20th); *Woman Chases Man* (Goldwyn-UA); *Another Dawn* (WB); *Ever Since Eve* (WB); *New Faces of 1937* (RKO); *Knight Without Armour* (Korda-UA); *The Toast of New York* (RKO); *Stella Dallas* (Goldwyn-UA); *Vogues of 1938* (UA); *The Prisoner of Zenda* (Selznick-UA); *Lost Horizon* (Col.); *Stage Door* (RKO); *Victoria the Great* (RKO); *The Awful Truth* (Col.); *Stand-In* (UA); *Nothing Sacred* (Selznick-UA); *I'll Take Romance* (Col.); and *Tovarich* (WB).

1938 *Snow White and the Seven Dwarfs* (Disney-RKO); *The Adventures of Tom Sawyer* (Selznick-UA); *Bringing Up Baby* (RKO); *Jezebel* (WB); *Fools for Scandal* (WB); *The Divorce of Lady X* (Korda-UA); *The Adventures of Marco Polo* (Goldwyn-UA); *There's Always a Woman* (Col.); *Joy of Living* (RKO); *The Adventures of Robin Hood* (WB); *Vivacious Lady* (RKO); *Blockade* (UA); *Holiday* (Col.); *Having Wonderful Time* (RKO); *Algiers* (UA); *Mother Carey's Chickens* (RKO); *Four's a Crowd* (WB); *Four Daughters* (WB); *You Can't Take It with You* (Col.); *Carefree* (RKO); *Drums* (Korda-UA); *There Goes My Heart* (UA); *The Mad Miss Manton* (RKO); *Young Dr. Kildare* (MGM); *The Young in Heart* (UA); *Sixty Glorious Years* (RKO); *The Cowboy and the Lady* (Goldwyn-UA); *Dramatic School* (MGM); *The Duke of West Point* (UA); *A Christmas Carol* (MGM); and *Topper Takes a Trip* (UA).

1939 *There's That Woman Again* (Col.); *Trade Winds* (UA); *The Great Man Votes* (RKO); *Gunga Din* (RKO); *Made for Each Other* (Selznick-UA); *Stagecoach* (UA); *Love Affair* (RKO); *The Story of Vernon and Irene Castle* (RKO); *Dark Victory* (WB); *East Side of Heaven* (Univ.); *Only Angels Have Wings* (Col.); *Captain Fury* (UA); *The Sun Never Sets* (Univ.); *Clouds over Europe* (Col.); *Good Girls Go to Paris* (Col.); *Bachelor Mother* (RKO); *The Man in the Iron Mask* (UA); *Winter Carnival* (UA); *In Name Only* (RKO); *Fifth Avenue Girl* (RKO); *Golden Boy* (Col.); *Nurse Edith Cavell* (RKO); *Intermezzo* (Selznick-UA); *Mr. Smith Goes to Washington* (Col.); *Ninotchka* (MGM); *We Are Not Alone* (WB); *Balalaika* (MGM); and *The Hunchback of Notre Dame* (RKO).

1940 *His Girl Friday* (Col.); *The Shop Around the Corner* (MGM); *Swiss Family Robinson* (RKO); *I Take This Woman* (MGM); *Abe Lincoln in Illinois* (RKO); *Too Many Husbands* (Col.); *Young Tom Edison* (MGM); *Rebecca* (Selznick-UA); *My Son, My Son!* (UA); *Irene* (RKO); *My Favorite Wife* (RKO); *Our Town* (UA); *Tom Brown's School Days* (RKO); *All This and Heaven Too* (WB); *South of Pago-Pago* (UA); *Pride and Prejudice* (MGM); *Lucky Partners* (RKO); *The Ramparts We Watch* (RKO); *The Howards of Virginia* (Col.); *They Knew What They Wanted* (RKO); *The Westerner* (Goldwyn-UA); *Escape* (MGM); *Bitter Sweet* (MGM); *The Thief of Baghdad* (Korda-UA); *No, No, Nanette* (RKO); and *The Philadelphia Story* (MGM).

1941 *This Thing Called Love* (Col.); *Mr. and Mrs. Smith* (RKO); *So Ends Our Night* (UA); *Cheers for Miss Bishop* (UA); *Adam Had Four Sons* (Col.); *That Hamilton Woman* (Korda-UA); *That Uncertain Feeling* (UA); *The Devil and Miss Jones* (RKO); *Penny Serenade* (Col.); *Sunny* (RKO); *She Knew All the Answers* (Col.); *Blossoms in the Dust* (MGM); *Tom, Dick and Harry* (RKO); *Here Comes Mr. Jordan* (Col.); *The Little Foxes* (Goldwyn-RKO); *Lydia* (Korda-UA); *It Started with Eve* (Univ.); *All That Money Can Buy* (RKO); *You'll Never Get Rich* (Col.); *Appointment for Love* (Univ.); *One Foot in Heaven* (WB); *Suspicion* (RKO); *The Men in Her Life* (Col.); *H. M. Pulham, Esq.* (MGM); and *Babes on Broadway* (MGM).

1942 *Ball of Fire* (Goldwyn-RKO); *Woman of the Year* (MGM); *Bedtime Story* (Col.); *Reap the Wild Wind* (Par.); *We Were Dancing* (MGM); *Saboteur* (Univ.); *Tortilla Flat* (MGM); *Mrs. Miniver* (MGM); *Bambi* (Disney-RKO); *The Talk of the Town* (Col.); *Tales of Manhattan* (20th); *My Sister Eileen* (Col.); *Once upon a Honeymoon* (RKO); *You Were Never Lovelier* (Col.); and *Random Harvest* (MGM).

1943 *They Got Me Covered* (Goldwyn-RKO); *Keeper of the Flame* (MGM); *Flight for Freedom* (RKO); *The More the Merrier* (Col.); *The Youngest Profession* (MGM); *So Proudly We Hail* (Par.); *Lassie Come Home* (MGM); *Claudia* (20th); *What a Woman* (Col.); and *Madame Curie* (MGM).

1944 *Jane Eyre* (20th); *Up in Arms* (Goldwyn-RKO); *Cover Girl* (Col.); *The White Cliffs of Dover* (MGM); *Once upon a Time* (Col.); *Dragon Seed* (MGM); *Casanova Brown* (RKO); *Mrs. Parkington* (MGM); *Together Again* (Col.); and *National Velvet* (MGM).

1945 *A Song to Remember* (Col.); *Tonight and Every Night* (Col.); *Without Love* (MGM); *The Valley of Decision* (MGM); *A Bell for Adano* (20th); *Over 21* (Col.); *Our Vines Have Tender Grapes* (MGM); *Weekend at the Waldorf* (MGM); and *The Bells of St. Mary's* (RKO).

1946 *Adventure* (MGM); *Gilda* (Col.); *The Green Years* (MGM); *To Each His Own* (Par.); *Anna and the King of Siam* (20th); *Notorious* (RKO); *The Jolson Story* (Col.); *Till the Clouds Roll By* (MGM); and *The Yearling* (MGM).

1947 *The Sea of Grass* (MGM); *The Late George Apley* (20th); *The Egg and I* (Univ.); *Great Expectations* (Univ.); *The Ghost and Mrs. Muir* (20th); *The Bachelor and the Bobby-Soxer* (RKO); *Down to Earth* (Col.); *Song of Love* (MGM); *Cass Timberlane* (MGM); *Good News* (MGM); and *A Double Life* (Univ.).

1948 *The Paradine Case* (Selznick); *I Remember Mama* (RKO); *State of the Union* (MGM); *The Pirate* (MGM); *The Emperor Waltz* (Par.); *A Date with Judy* (MGM); *Good Sam* (RKO); *Julia Misbehaves* (MGM); *You Gotta Stay Happy* (Univ.); *Hills of Home* (MGM); and *Words and Music* (MGM).

1949 *A Letter to Three Wives* (20th); *Family Honeymoon* (Univ.); *Little Women* (MGM); *A Connecticut Yankee in King Arthur's Court* (Par.); *The Stratton Story* (MGM); *Edward My Son* (MGM); *Look for the Silver Lining* (WB); *In the Good Old Summertime* (MGM); *Under Capricorn* (WB); *The Heiress* (Par.); *That Forsyte Woman* (MGM); *On the Town* (MGM); and *My Foolish Heart* (Goldwyn-RKO).

1950 *Young Man with a Horn* (WB); *Stage Fright* (WB); *A Woman of Distinction* (Col.); *The Daughter of Rosie O'Grady* (WB); *No Sad Songs for Me* (Col.); *Father of the Bride* (MGM); *The Next Voice You Hear* (MGM); *The Men* (UA); *Sunset Boulevard* (Par.); *The Glass Menagerie* (WB); *The Miniver Story* (MGM); *King Solomon's Mines* (MGM); *Kim* (MGM); and *The Magnificent Yankee* (MGM).

1951 *September Affair* (Par.); *Payment on Demand* (RKO); *Royal Wedding* (MGM); *Father's Little Dividend* (MGM); *The Great Caruso* (MGM); *Show Boat* (MGM); *Captain Horatio Hornblower* (WB); *An American in Paris* (MGM); *Too Young to Kiss* (MGM); and *I'll See You in My Dreams* (WB).

1952 *The Greatest Show on Earth* (Par.); *Singin' in the Rain* (MGM); *Scaramouche* (MGM); *Lovely to Look At* (MGM); *Where's Charley* (WB); *Ivanhoe* (MGM); *Because You're Mine* (MGM); *The Happy Time* (Col.); *Plymouth Adventure* (MGM); *Million Dollar Mermaid* (MGM); and *The Bad and the Beautiful* (MGM).

1953 *Tonight We Sing* (20th); *The Story of Three Loves* (MGM); *By the Light of the Silvery Moon* (WB); *Shane* (Par.); *Young Bess* (MGM); *Dangerous When Wet* (MGM); *The Band Wagon* (MGM); *Roman Holiday* (Par.); *Mogambo* (MGM); *Kiss Me Kate* (MGM); and *Easy to Love* (MGM).

1954 *Knights of the Round Table* (MGM); *The Long, Long Trailer* (MGM); *Rhapsody* (MGM); *Rose Marie* (MGM); *Executive Suite* (MGM); *The Student Prince* (MGM); *Seven Brides for Seven Brothers* (MGM); *Brigadoon* (MGM); *White Christmas* (Par.); and *Deep in My Heart* (MGM).

1955 *The Bridges at Toko-Ri* (Par.); *Jupiter's Darling* (MGM); *Hit the Deck* (MGM); *The Glass Slipper* (MGM); *Interrupted Melody* (MGM); *Love Me or Leave Me* (MGM); *Mister Roberts* (WB); *It's Always Fair Weather* (MGM); *Trial* (MGM); *The Tender Trap* (MGM); *Kismet* (MGM); *I'll Cry Tomorrow* (MGM); and *Picnic* (Col.).

1956 *Serenade* (WB); *The Swan* (MGM); *Bhowani Junction* (MGM); *The Eddie Duchin Story* (Col.); *High Society* (MGM); *Tea and Sympathy* (MGM); *Friendly Persuasion* (Allied Artists); and *The Teahouse of the August Moon* (MGM).

1957 *The Barretts of Wimpole Street* (MGM); *The Wings of Eagles* (MGM); *The Spirit of St. Louis* (WB); *Funny Face* (Par.); *Designing Woman* (MGM); *The Prince and the Showgirl* (WB); *Silk Stockings* (MGM); *The Pajama Game* (WB); *Les Girls* (MGM); *Don't Go Near the Water* (MGM); and *Sayonara* (WB).

1958 *Seven Hills of Rome* (MGM); *The Brothers Karamazov* (MGM); *Merry Andrew* (MGM); *Marjorie Morningstar* (WB); *No Time for Sergeants* (WB); *Indiscreet* (WB); *The Reluctant Debutante* (MGM); *Cat on a Hot Tin Roof* (MGM); *Home Before Dark* (WB); *Auntie Mame* (WB); and *Some Came Running* (MGM).

1959 *The Journey* (MGM); *Green Mansions* (MGM); *Count Your Blessings* (MGM); *Ask Any Girl* (MGM); *The Nun's Story* (WB); *North by Northwest* (MGM); *The FBI Story* (WB); *A Summer Place* (WB); *The Miracle* (WB); and *Operation Petticoat* (Univ.).

1960 *Never So Few* (MGM); *Once More with Feeling* (Col.); *Home from the Hill* (MGM); *Please Don't Eat the Daisies* (MGM); *Pollyana* (Disney-BV); *Bells Are Ringing* (MGM); *Song Without End* (Col.); *The Dark at the Top of the Stairs* (WB); *Midnight Lace* (Univ.); *The World of Suzie Wong* (Par.); and *The Sundowners* (WB).

1961 *Where the Boys Are* (MGM); *Cimarron* (MGM); *The Absent-Minded Professor* (Disney-BV); *Parrish* (WB); *The Pleasure of His Company* (Par.); *Fanny* (WB); *Come September* (Univ.); *Breakfast at Tiffany's* (Par.); *Flower Drum Song* (Univ.); and *Babes in Toyland* (Disney-BV).

1962 *A Majority of One* (WB); *Lover Come Back* (Univ.); *Rome Adventure* (WB); *Moon Pilot* (Disney-BV); *Bon Voyage!* (Disney-BV); *That Touch of Mink* (Univ.); *The Music Man* (WB); *Gigot* (20th); *Jumbo* (MGM); *Days of Wine and Roses* (WB); and *To Kill a Mockingbird* (Univ.).

1963 *A Girl Named Tamiko* (Par.); *Bye Bye Birdie* (Col.); *Spencer's Mountain* (WB); *Come Blow Your Horn* (Par.);

The Thrill of It All (Univ.); *The VIPs* (MGM); *Mary, Mary* (WB); *The Wheeler Dealers* (MGM); and *Charade* (Univ.).

1964 *The Prize* (MGM); *Captain Newman, M.D.* (Univ.); *The World of Henry Orient* (UA); *The Pink Panther* (UA); *The Chalk Garden* (Univ.); *The Unsinkable Molly Brown* (MGM); *Mary Poppins* (Disney-BV); *Send Me No Flowers* (Univ.); and *Father Goose* (Univ.).

1965 *36 Hours* (MGM); *Dear Heart* (WB); *Operation Crossbow* (MGM); *The Yellow Rolls Royce* (MGM); *The Sandpiper* (MGM); *The Great Race* (WB); *Never Too Late* (WB); and *That Darn Cat* (Disney-BV).

1966 *Judith* (Par.); *Inside Daisy Clover* (WB); *The Singing Nun* (MGM); *Arabesque* (Univ.); *The Glass Bottom Boat* (MGM); *How to Steal a Million* (20th); *Kaleidoscope* (WB); *Any Wednesday* (WB); *Penelope* (MGM); and *Follow the Boys* (MGM).

1967 *Hotel* (WB); *The 25th Hour* (MGM); *How to Succeed in Business Without Really Trying* (UA); *Two for the Road* (20th); *Barefoot in the Park* (Par.); *Up the Down Staircase* (WB); *The Bobo* (WB); *Wait Until Dark* (WB); and *The Happiest Millionaire* (Disney-BV).

1968 *How to Save a Marriage—And Ruin Your Life* (Col.); *Sweet November* (WB); *The Secret War of Harry Frigg* (Univ.); *The One and Only Genuine Original Family Band* (Disney-BV); *The Odd Couple* (Par.); *Where Were You When the Lights Went Out?* (MGM); *Hot Millions* (MGM); *Bullitt* (WB); and *The Impossible Years* (MGM).

1969 *The Brotherhood* (Par.); *Mayerling* (MGM); *The Love Bug* (Disney-BV); *If It's Tuesday, This Must Be Belgium* (UA); *Winning* (Univ.); *True Grit* (Par.); *The Gypsy Moths* (MGM); *The Christmas Tree* (Continental); *Hail, Hero!* (Cinema Center); *The Brain* (Par.); and *A Boy Named Charlie Brown* (Cinema Center).

1970 *Viva Max* (Comm. United); *. . . Tick . . . Tick . . . Tick* (MGM); *Airport* (Univ.); *The Out-of-Towners* (Par.); *Darling Lili* (Par.); *Sunflower* (Avco-Embassy); *The Private Lives of Sherlock Holmes* (US); and *Scrooge* (Cinema Center).

1971 *Promise at Dawn* (Avco-Embassy); *Wuthering Heights* (A.I.P.); *A New Leaf* (Par.); *Plaza Suite* (Par.); *Murphy's War* (Par.); *The Red Tent* (Par.); *See No Evil* (Col.); *Kotch* (ABC/Cinerama); *The Railway Children* (Univ.); and *Bedknobs and Broomsticks* (Disney-BV).

1972 *The Cowboys* (WB); *Mary, Queen of Scots* (Univ.); *What's Up, Doc?* (WB); *Play It Again, Sam* (Par.); *The War Between Men and Women* (Cinema Center); *Butterflies Are Free* (Col.); *Last of the Red Hot Lovers* (Par.); *Cancel My Reservation* (WB); *When the Legends Die* (20th); and *1776* (Col.).

1973 *The World's Greatest Athlete* (Disney-BV); *Charlotte's Web* (Par.); *Tom Sawyer* (WB); *Mary Poppins* (Disney-BV); *Forty Carats* (Col.); *Night Watch* (Avco-Embassy); *The Mixed-Up World of Mrs. Basil E. Frankweiler* (Cinema 5); *The Optimists* (Par.); and *The Adventures of Robin Hood* (Disney-BV).

1974 *Superdad* (Disney-BV); *Mame* (WB); *The Black Windmill* (Univ.); *Herbie Rides Again* (Disney-BV); *The Tamarind Seed* (Avco-Embassy); *The Girl from Petrovka* (Univ.); and *The Little Prince* (Par.).

1975 *At Long Last Love* (20th); *Gone with the Wind* (Selznick-MGM); *2001: A Space Odyssey* (MGM); *Singin' in the Rain* (MGM); *Doctor Zhivago* (MGM); *The Wind and the Lion* (MGM); *Bite the Bullet* (Col.); *Hennessy* (AIP); and *The Sunshine Boys* (MGM).

1976 *Robin and Marian* (Col.); *Blue Bird* (20th); *1776* (Col.); *Harry and Walter Go to New York* (Col.); *Swashbuckler* (Univ.); *A Matter of Time* (AIP); and *The Slipper and the Rose* (Univ.).

1977 *Mr. Billion* (20th); *The Sting* (Univ.); *Smokey and the Bandit* (Univ.); *MacArthur* (Univ.); and *Pete's Dragon* (Disney-BV).

1978 *Crossed Swords* (WB); *Sea Gypsies* (WB); *Fantasia* (Disney-BV); *Matilda* (AIP); *Magic of Lassie* (Wrather Corp.). *Caravans* (Univ.).

INDEX

Author Charles Francisco soaks up "inspiration" in the Music Hall's green room with the help of Rockettes Pam Kelleher (left) and Dee Dee Knapp. (Photo by Vito Torelli.)

Charles Francisco began his professional writing career at the age of fifteen as a sportswriter on *The Evening Courier* in his home town of Champaign-Urbana, Illinois. He continued that work until his success as an actor in productions at the University of Illinois prompted his faculty advisors to encourage him to seek a career in the theater. He has managed success in both fields.

He has starred opposite a number of celebrated leading ladies in stage productions in New York, Chicago, Los Angeles, and elsewhere, and was featured on some forty of Hollywood's most successful television series during the 1960s. He came East to do a play in 1967 and decided to stay when he was offered a job as News Director on one of New York's top-rated radio stations. He left broadcasting a couple of years ago to devote full time to serious writing.

His journalism assignments have ranged from political analysis to drama criticism. Chuck was also a highly-decorated Army Combat Correspondent during the Korean War. His article "A GI's View of the War" was nationally syndicated in Drew Pearson's *Washington Merry-Go-Round* column in 1951.

As for future plans, Francisco says, "I'd like to find another project as interesting as this one has been. I also want to finish a novel I've been working on and buy a house in Ireland—where even the warriors are poets."